WATERLOO PUBLIC LIBRARY

W9-CCZ-434

Second Edition

ORGANIZING SUCCESSFUL TOURNAMENTS

JOHN BYL, PhD

Redeemer College
Ancaster, Ontario

WATERLOO PUBLIC LIBRARY

Human Kinetics

Library of Congress Cataloging-in-Publication Data

Byl, John.
    Organizing successful tournaments / by John Byl. -- 2nd ed.
      p.   cm.
    ISBN 0-88011-955-1
    1. Sports administration.   2. Tournaments--Management.   I. Title.
    GV713.B95   1998
    796'.06'9--dc21   98-11714
                                              CIP

ISBN: 0-88011-955-1

Copyright © 1990 by Human Kinetics Publishers
Copyright © 1999 by John Byl

All rights reserved. Except for use in a review, the reproduction or utilization of this work in any form or by any electronic, mechanical, or other means, now known or hereafter invented, including xerography, photocopying, and recording, and in any information storage and retrieval system, is forbidden without the written permission of the publisher.

Notice: Permission to reproduce the following material is granted to instructors and agencies who have purchased *Organizing Successful Tournaments, second edition:* pp. 20-33, 43-53, 65-78, 96, 145-147, 157, 161-163, and 168. The reproduction of other parts of this book is expressly forbidden by the above copyright notice. Persons or agencies who have not purchased *Organizing Successful Tournaments, second edition* may not reproduce any material.

Acquisitions Editor: Jim Kestner; **Managing Editor:** Melinda Graham; **Copyeditor:** Denelle Eknes; **Proofreader:** Lisa Satterthwaite; **Graphic Designer:** Nancy Rasmus; **Graphic Artist:** Kathleen Boudreau-Fuoss; **Illustrators:** Joe Bellis and Kathleen Boudreau-Fuoss; **Cover Designer:** Jack Davis; **Printer:** United Graphics

Human Kinetics books are available at special discounts for bulk purchase. Special editions or book excerpts can also be created to specification. For details, contact the Special Sales Manager at Human Kinetics.

Printed in the United States of America   10 9 8 7 6 5 4 3

Human Kinetics
Web site: www.humankinetics.com

United States: Human Kinetics, P.O. Box 5076, Champaign, IL 61825-5076
800-747-4457
e-mail: humank@hkusa.com

Canada: Human Kinetics, 475 Devonshire Road, Unit 100, Windsor, ON N8Y 2L5
800-465-7301 (in Canada only)
e-mail: orders@hkcanada.com

Europe: Human Kinetics, Units C2/C3 Wira Business Park, West Park Ring Road
Leeds LS16 6EB, United Kingdom
+44 (0) 113 278 1708
e-mail: hk@hkeurope.com

Australia: Human Kinetics, 57A Price Avenue, Lower Mitcham, South Australia 5062
08 8277 1555
e-mail: liahka@senet.com.au

New Zealand: Human Kinetics, P.O. Box 105-231, Auckland Central
09-523-3462
e-mail: hkp@ihug.co.nz

CONTENTS

Preface   v

Acknowledgments   vii

Chapter 1   Types and Selection of Tournaments   **1**

Tournament Types   2

Tournament Selection   4

Seeding and Byes   8

Using the Draw Sheets   16

Chapter 2   Single-Elimination Tournament   **17**

Draw Sheets   20

Playing Schedules   34

Chapter 3   Multilevel Tournament   **39**

Draw Sheets   43

Playing Schedules   54

Chapter 4   Double-Elimination Tournament   **61**

Draw Sheets   65

Playing Schedules   79

Chapter 5   Round Robin Tournament   **85**

Round Robin-Double Split   87

Round Robin-Triple Split   89

Round Robin-Quadruple Split   90

Playing Schedules for Round Robin Tournaments   97

Playing Schedules for Round Robin-Double Split Tournaments 109

Playing Schedules for Round Robin-Triple Split Tournaments 121

Playing Schedules for Round Robin-Quadruple Split Tournaments 129

Chapter 6 Extended Tournaments 135

Ladder Tournament 136

Pyramid Tournament 136

Level Rotation 137

Tournament Construction 140

Chapter 7 Large Tournaments 141

Pool Sheets 145

Chapter 8 Seeding and Byes 149

Byes 150

Seeding 150

Chapter 9 Planning and Conducting Tournaments 155

Avoiding Problems 156

Committee Responsibilities 159

The Tournament Director and the Law 160

Appendix: Tiebreaking Procedures 165

Tiebreaking Procedures for Games 165

Tiebreaking Procedures for Tournaments 168

Glossary 173

About the Author 174

PREFACE

■ This book is intended to help you organize well-run tournaments with the greatest of ease. Whether you are a physical educator, a coach, a director of athletics, or in charge of intramurals, you often use tournaments to help organize people at play. Have you and I not often experienced the frustrations that organizing and participating in tournaments sometimes bring with them? Has it not often occurred that leaders have avoided using a tournament structure because its preparation was too time-consuming? How often has one organized a tournament only to find that a player or team has dropped out at the last minute? How often has it happened that halfway through a tournament an error was found in the schedule, and confusion reigned? How often has it happened that one or two teams played most of their games on the worst court or field? And how often has one felt frustrated because the tournament format eliminated poor players too quickly, or because the tournament took too long or had too many games? I daresay that most of us have experienced these situations.

This manual is designed to alleviate some of the above problems and to assist you, the tournament director, in several ways. The most commonly used tournaments are presented in this book, including Single and Double Elimination, Multilevel, four different Round Robins, and several extended tournaments such as the Ladder or Pyramid.

Chapter 1 explains the major strengths and weaknesses of each type of tournament. This should help you select the tournament that best suits your goals. Once you have selected the most appropriate tournament type, you simply need to turn to the chapter specifically devoted to your preferred tournament, where you will find your work made considerably easier. Each chapter begins with an explanation of relevant details involved in implementing a particular tournament. A seeding chart is also provided to ensure the best possible quality of play. Finally, the actual draw sheets and the playing schedules for the relevant number of playing areas are included. Once you have selected a tournament, a ranking of the participants should be completed; participants' names are then placed on the draw sheet according to the seeding table, and the schedule is ready and play can begin. Your problem-free tournament is prepared simply and quickly.

For all tournaments, but especially for major ones, a chapter on planning and conducting tournaments has been included that covers such details as organizing committees to handle awards, officiating, and accommodations. A time line is also presented to ensure that all is ready when the tournament starts. Tiebreaking procedures for different sports and tournaments are provided to help deal with those very close games.

I wish you well in your important and exciting role as tournament director.

To Mom and Dad,
thanks for your love and support.

ACKNOWLEDGMENTS

This book was made possible through the assistance of several institutions and people. I first wish to thank Redeemer College and its support community for making it possible for me to work on this book. In particular I would like to thank Jeannette Grasman, who helped with a lot of the more tedious computer entries and calculations.

I am also very appreciative of the work that Human Kinetics is doing and the kind of support they are providing for those involved in physical education and sport. Their careful assistance in the production of this book is also appreciated.

The chapter on extended tournaments borrowed from Boyden and Burton's book *Staging Successful Tournaments*. Permission to use their work is appreciated.

I wish to thank my wife, Catherine, who, in the preparation of this book and always, has given so much to me in so many different ways. My children Hannah, Judith, Matthew, and Charis have also given of their time with me, and I thank them for their love.

C H A P T E R 1

Types and Selection of Tournaments

■ The reasons for you, the tournament director, to organize people at play in a tournament or league are varied. Most often we use tournaments to determine the ranking of participants or to provide a structure within which ranking is possible. You will undoubtedly have subgoals, which will be affected by the availability of time and facilities. With respect to your subgoals, you must clearly answer questions such as these: Do I want all players to play an equal number of games? Does it matter whether the number of games is the same per player? Do I want all the games to be closely contested? Does it matter if there are a few lopsided games? How important is it to know who comes in first, second, third, fourth, or fifth? The answers to these questions will help you decide which tournament type to use.

Time and facilities sometimes will limit your options, and you may need some compromises. You must have a realistic assessment of the number of games required for various tournament types and of the time it would take to complete a tournament with the number of playing areas available. It is important, however, that you first establish goals for your tournament, then determine how realistic these goals are in terms of time and facilities. If you need to compromise, keep close to your goals. Helpful evaluations of each tournament type follow, and table 1.1 on page 5 summarizes this information.

Once you complete this decision-making process, the remaining work is straightforward. Turn to the appropriate chapter, find the draw sheet for the required number of entries, and photocopy it. Seed entries and place their names on the draw sheet as suggested by the seeding tables in the same chapter. We provide schedules for the relevant number of playing areas, and you should select the appropriate one.

Tournament Types

To make it easier to select the appropriate tournament type, we list the highlights of each. We include the strengths and weaknesses of each tournament type, as well as suggestions for the best use for each tournament.

Single Elimination

The greatest appeal of the single-elimination tournament is its simplicity. Losers are eliminated, and winners advance to the next round until there is only one contestant left, the tournament champion. The single-elimination tourney is valuable when the number of entries is large, time is short, and the number of playing areas is limited. Of all the tournaments, this one requires the fewest games; however, half the participants are eliminated after one game, and only one-quarter of the participants remain after the second round. When more extensive participation is important and more playing areas and time are available, using this tourney is not advisable. Furthermore, you can easily organize other tournaments in this manual, so the simplicity of single elimination is not a significant factor in its favor.

Probably the best use for this type of tournament is play-offs at the end of a season or following a longer tournament such as a split round robin. You would then determine seeding for the single elimination by the standings at the conclusion of the previous playing period.

Double Elimination

The double-elimination tournament is designed to address two problems inherent in the single-elimination tournament. The first is that one of the best entries may have a bad first game or have been poorly seeded in the single-elimination draw; if that occurs in a single-elimination tournament, that entry is eliminated too soon. Having a losers' bracket gives such an entry an opportunity to play in the finals. The second problem with the single elimination is that half of the entries play only one game. The double elimination ensures that all entries play at least two games.

However, this tournament type is often overrated because of those strengths. It also has weaknesses, and there are good alternatives. The major difficulties with the double elimination are that the second- and third-seeded players play many games, particularly in the final rounds of the tournament, and it takes many rounds to complete. Also, this tournament type often does not use available areas efficiently. For example, if the tournament consists of nine entries and there are four playing areas available, the double-elimination tournament takes seven rounds to complete. This is as many rounds as in a round robin-double split, but without the advantages a round robin tournament offers.

The double elimination's major benefit is for situations in which the number of playing areas is limited, time is at a premium, final standings are important, and all entries are to be awarded a minimum of two games.

Multilevel

The multilevel tournament is similar to a single-elimination tournament; in fact, at the top level they are the same. However, in multilevel a player is not eliminated following a loss but simply moves down one or more levels of play into the consolation rounds. This downward movement continues until no other challengers remain. One result of this approach is that all players play about the same number of games. Another benefit is that in each round the players are more likely to encounter others of their caliber.

In the final rounds of play in single- and double-elimination tournaments, there are only one or two playing areas in use. This is not the case in the multilevel tournament. As a result, when sufficient playing areas are available, the multilevel tournament takes the same time to complete as a single-elimination tournament and half the time of a double-elimination tournament. For example, if six playing areas are available and the tournament contains 13 entries, it takes four rounds to complete the tournament using either the single elimination or the multilevel and eight rounds to complete a double elimination. The multilevel tournament is an excellent choice when equality in number of games played and closely contested matches are important considerations, when time is limited, and when a knowledge of third and subsequent final placements is not crucial.

This tournament is perhaps most useful in physical education classes or intramural or recreational settings where eliminating players is undesirable and final standings are of little significance. Because this tournament type offers many advantages in these situations, and because it may be new to the reader, we advise a review of chapter 3.

Round Robin

The round robin tournament consists of all individuals or teams playing each entry an equal number of times. The round robin and round robin-split tournaments listed here have fixed schedules; all entries know exactly who they play and what time they play them, which offers some advantage to entries in preparing for the tournament and upcoming games. Seeding does not affect the outcome, because the cumulative results of all games played determine final standings. When the number of entries are few and games are played quickly (as in table tennis, badminton, or volleyball), this type of format is effective for a one-day tournament. When there are more entries and the games take longer to complete (as in hockey, football, or basketball), then a round robin schedule is best suited for league play. In this case, one time through a round robin provides the league schedule, and, if time permits, you could provide a home and away schedule simply by going through the round robin schedule twice.

The round robin format is not suitable for all situations. Because all entries play each other, a round robin format is problematic when the number of entries is high. For example, a tournament with 32 entries would take 496 games to complete using a round robin. This compares with 62 games in a double elimination and only 31 in single elimination. Also, when there is considerable discrepancy in caliber of play, many games will prove unsatisfactory to all involved in these (non)contests.

Round Robin-Double Split

When a round robin format is desirable but the number of entries is too large, splitting the entries into two pools is a practical solution. Following the play within the pools, only the top two entries from each pool participate in play-offs to determine the final top standings. The obvious benefit is that the number of games is halved. The drawback is that proper seeding becomes important. For example, if the top three seeds are placed in one pool and only the top two from each pool advance to the play-offs, then (if entries perform consistent with their seedings) the third seed cannot play in the play-offs.

This format is commonly used for league play. You could split the league into two pools or divisions, with the play-offs bringing together the top two teams from each division to decide final standings.

Round Robin-Triple Split

The round robin-triple split is similar to the double split. However, because it would be awkward to have a single-elimination play-off with three or six finalists, a round robin format for the finalists is the most suitable. This requires more games in the play-offs and is a satisfactory alternative to the double split only when there is a very large number of entries.

Round Robin-Quadruple Split

This type of tournament is intended to solve the same problems addressed by the double split, but instead of dividing the entries into two groups, they are divided into four groups. This is useful only when the number of entries exceeds 11. You could use it in a one- or two-day tournament or in a league format over a longer time. The major disadvantage of this approach is that when there are only 12 to 15 entries, the weaker ones might participate in only two games.

Extended

Ladder and pyramid tournaments are two common examples of this tournament type. Extended tournaments can be ongoing for an indefinite time or can be abbreviated to a week, a month, or another desired period. For drop-in programs, such as intramurals or racquet clubs, this tournament type can be most useful. Its major weaknesses are, first, that players challenge each other and, therefore, some players may not play as much, and, second, because of the challenge system the ranking at the end of the tournament may not be accurate.

Tournament Selection

There are five important variables to consider when planning a tournament: the number of games required to complete a tournament, equality of the numbers of games entries will be participating in, how long the tournament will last, how close most of the games will be, and how important accuracy of seeding is to a well-run tournament. Using these variables, table 1.1 evaluates each tournament type in this book.

If you are pressed for time and have only one playing area, a single-elimination format will always be the quickest way of completing a tournament. However, if

Table 1.1 Tournament Selection Guide

	Number of games	Equal number of games for all entries	Time to complete tournament if many playing areas are available	Number of nonclose games	Importance of accurate seeding
Single Elimination	Very few	Very poor	Short	Many	Very important
Double Elimination	Few	Poor	Long	Few	Important
Multilevel	Few	Good	Short	Very few	Very important
Round Robin	Very many	Very good	Very long	Many	Not very important
Round Robin – Double Split	Many	Good	Long	Many	Important
Round Robin – Triple Split	Many	Good	Very long	Many	Important
Round Robin – Quadruple Split	Few	Good	Long	Many	Important
Extended	Optional	Possible	Optional	Many	Not very important

you have more playing sites available, single-elimination's time advantage is minimized. Table 1.2 identifies how many rounds it takes to complete tournaments of various sizes using a number of playing areas.

Various assumptions are built into these calculations. In double elimination it is assumed that the number one seed does not lose any matches. For round robin-split tournaments, the top two finishers of each pool advanced to the play-offs, and we have also included a game for third and fourth place. Therefore, the play-off round requires four extra games for the double split, six extra games for the triple split, and eight games for the quadruple split.

When reading the table, the first column under "1" playing area also equals the total number of games required for the tournament. This reference chart is intended to supply the tournament organizer with information about the number of rounds it takes to complete a tournament. This information helps the tournament convener weigh the personal goals with time and facility requirements.

You can observe from the table that single-elimination and double-elimination tournaments use multiple playing sites least effectively, that the round robin-split tournaments use these sites reasonably well, and that multilevel and round robin tournaments use available sites most efficiently.

The following example illustrates how you can use the table. If there were eight entries and only one playing area, single elimination would be the quickest format to complete. However, if you had four playing areas, it would take just as long to

Table 1.2 Rounds to Complete Tournament

	Number of playing areas							
	1	**2**	**3**	**4**	**5**	**6**	**7**	**8**
Two entries								
SE	1							
Three entries								
SE	2							
DE	4							
RR	3							
Four entries								
SE	3	2						
DE	6	4						
RR	6	3						
Five entries								
SE	4	3						
DE	8	5						
RR	10	5						
Six entries								
SE	5	3	3					
ML	7	4	3					
DE	10	6	6					
RR	15	8	5					
RD	10	5	5					
Seven entries								
SE	6	4	3					
ML	9	5	3					
DE	12	7	6					
RR	21	11	7					
RD	13	7	5					
Eight entries								
SE	7	4	4	3				
ML	12	6	5	3				
DE	14	8	7	6				
RR	28	14	10	7				
RD	16	8	6	5				
Nine entries								
SE	8	5	4	4				
ML	14	7	5	4				
DE	16	9	8	7				
RR	36	18	12	9				
RD	20	10	8	7				
RT	15	8	8	8				
Ten entries								
SE	9	5	4	4	4			
ML	15	8	5	4	4			
DE	18	10	8	7	7			
RR	45	23	15	12	9			
RD	24	12	9	7	7			
RT	15	9	7	6	6			

			Number of playing areas					
	1	**2**	**3**	**4**	**5**	**6**	**7**	**8**
Eleven entries								
SE	10	6	5	4	4			
ML	17	9	6	5	4			
DE	20	11	9	8	8			
RR	55	28	19	14	11			
RD	29	15	11	9	7			
RT	21	11	8	7	6			
Twelve entries								
SE	11	6	5	4	4	4		
ML	20	10	7	5	5	5		
DE	22	12	10	8	8	8		
RR	66	33	17	14	11	11		
RD	34	17	12	10	8	7		
RT	24	12	9	8	7	6		
RQ	20	10	8	6	6	6		
Thirteen entries								
SE	12	7	5	5	4	4		
ML	22	11	8	6	5	4		
DE	24	13	10	9	8	8		
RR	78	39	26	20	16	13		
RD	40	20	14	11	10	9		
RT	28	14	11	9	8	7		
RQ	23	12	9	7	6	6		
Fourteen entries								
SE	13	8	6	5	5	4	4	
ML	25	13	9	7	5	5	4	
DE	26	14	11	9	9	8	8	
RR	91	46	31	23	19	16	13	
RD	46	23	16	13	11	9	9	
RT	32	16	12	10	9	8	8	
RQ	26	13	10	8	7	6	6	
Fifteen entries								
SE	14	8	6	5	5	5	4	
ML	28	14	10	7	6	6	4	
DE	28	15	12	10	9	9	8	
RR	105	53	35	27	21	18	15	
RD	53	27	19	15	12	11	9	
RT	36	19	13	11	9	8	8	
RQ	29	15	11	9	8	7	6	
Sixteen entries								
SE	15	8	6	5	5	5	5	4
ML	32	15	10	8	7	6	5	4
DE	32	17	12	10	10	9	9	8
RR	120	60	40	30	24	20	18	15
RD	60	30	21	16	14	12	10	9
RT	41	21	15	12	10	9	8	8
RQ	32	16	12	9	8	8	7	6

complete a single-elimination tournament as it would to complete a multilevel tournament (three rounds), and only two additional rounds to complete a round robin-double split tournament (five rounds).

Seeding and Byes

Seeding and byes are important concepts to understand in preparing a successful tournament. Chapter 8 will help you understand how to place byes and how to seed in a variety of tournaments. This section briefly defines seeding and byes and indicates how you can implement these concepts using this manual.

Seeding

Seeding is defined as the process of ranking players before the tournament according to their relative ability. The main principle, especially for an elimination tournament, is that the top two entries should meet in the final game; the logical extension of this is that the higher an entry is ranked, the closer it should come to the final game before being eliminated. A second principle, which is applied differently depending on the seeding philosophy, is that it should be equally difficult for entries of similar ability to achieve similar ends. Let's quickly illustrate this point with a tournament of 16 entries. Using the equitable seeding approach, the 1st seed competes with the 11th seed and the 2nd seed competes with the 12th seed, both 10 seeds apart. Using the advantage seeding approach, the 1st seed competes with the 16th, and the 2nd seed competes with the 15th; the higher seed playing the easiest competitor, the 2nd seed playing the 2nd easiest competitor.

Figure 1.1 illustrates how seeding works using the equitable seeding approach, showing a draw sheet for a single elimination with five entries. Seed number five should be eliminated first because it should be the weakest entry. In the second round, the third and fourth seeds should be eliminated, and in the final round the second seed should be eliminated, leaving the top seed victorious.

The number of rounds gives important but only partial information. It is also helpful to know how different tournament types impact the number of games

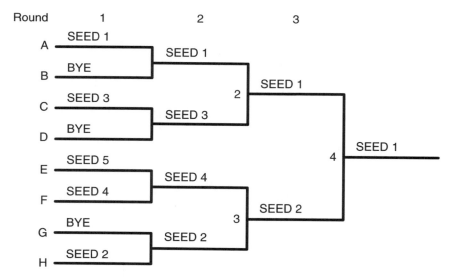

Figure 1.1 Single elimination—five entries.

each entry can expect. For example, one goal of many tournaments, especially in recreational settings, is to equalize the number of games each entry plays. Often this goal needs to be compromised due to limited playing time or the importance of determining overall rankings. The purpose of table 1.3 is to provide data on the number of games required for seven common tournament types. This information will assist the tournament director in selecting the tournament best suited to the tournament goals.

A discussion of the play-off structure used to calculate the number of games for each tournament follows. The double elimination (DE) data was calculated assuming the first place team lost no matches. Round robin-double split (RD) was calculated assuming a four-game play-off format with the top four teams. The

Table 1.3 Seeded Position Combinations

	SE	DE	ML	RR	RD	RT	RQ
Three entries							
Seeded position 1	1	2		2			
Seeded position 2	2	4		2			
Seeded position 3	1	2		2			
Total	2.00	4.00		3.00			
Maximum	2.00	4.00		2.00			
Minimum	1.00	2.00		2.00			
Mean	1.33	2.67		2.00			
Four entries							
Seeded position 1	2	3		3			
Seeded position 2	2	4		3			
Seeded position 3	1	3		3			
Seeded position 4	1	2		3			
Total	3.00	6.00		6.00			
Maximum	2.00	4.00		3.00			
Minimum	1.00	2.00		3.00			
Mean	1.50	3.00		3.00			
Five entries							
Seeded position 1	2	3		5			
Seeded position 2	2	4		4			
Seeded position 3	1	4		4			
Seeded position 4	2	3		4			
Seeded position 5	1	2		4			
Total	4.00	8.00		10.00			
Maximum	2.00	4.00		4.00			
Minimum	1.00	2.00		4.00			
Mean	1.60	3.20		4.00			
Six entries							
Seeded position 1	2	3	2	5	4		
Seeded position 2	2	4	2	5	4		
Seeded position 3	2	5	3	5	4		
Seeded position 4	2	4	3	5	4		

(continued)

Table 1.3   *(continued)*

	SE	DE	ML	RR	RD	RT	RQ
Seeded position 5	1	2	2	5	2		
Seeded position 6	1	2	2	5	2		
Total	5.00	10.00	7.00	15.00	10.00		
Maximum	2.00	5.00	3.00	5.00	4.00		
Minimum	1.00	2.00	2.00	5.00	2.00		
Mean	1.67	3.33	2.33	5.00	3.33		
Seven entries							
Seeded position 1	2	3	2	6	4		
Seeded position 2	3	5	3	6	5		
Seeded position 3	2	5	3	6	4		
Seeded position 4	2	4	3	6	5		
Seeded position 5	1	2	2	6	2		
Seeded position 6	1	3	3	6	3		
Seeded position 7	1	2	2	6	3		
Total	6.00	12.00	9.00	21.00	13.00		
Maximum	3.00	5.00	3.00	6.00	5.00		
Minimum	1.00	2.00	2.00	6.00	3.00		
Mean	1.71	3.43	2.57	6.00	3.71		
Eight entries							
Seeded position 1	3	4	3	7	5		
Seeded position 2	3	5	3	7	5		
Seeded position 3	2	5	3	7	5		
Seeded position 4	2	4	3	7	5		
Seeded position 5	1	3	3	7	3		
Seeded position 6	1	3	3	7	3		
Seeded position 7	1	2	3	7	3		
Seeded position 8	1	2	3	7	3		
Total	7.00	14.00	12.00	28.00	16.00		
Maximum	3.00	5.00	3.00	7.00	5.00		
Minimum	1.00	2.00	3.00	7.00	3.00		
Mean	1.75	3.50	3.00	7.00	4.00		
Nine entries							
Seeded position 1	3	4	3	8	5	7	
Seeded position 2	3	5	3	8	6	7	
Seeded position 3	2	5	3	8	5	7	
Seeded position 4	2	4	4	8	6	7	
Seeded position 5	1	3	3	8	3	7	
Seeded position 6	1	4	3	8	4	7	
Seeded position 7	1	2	3	8	3	2	
Seeded position 8	2	3	3	8	4	2	
Seeded position 9	1	2	3	8	4	2	
Total	8.00	16.00	14.00	36.00	20.00	24.00	
Maximum	3.00	5.00	4.00	8.00	6.00	7.00	
Minimum	1.00	2.00	3.00	8.00	3.00	3.00	
Mean	1.78	3.56	3.11	8.00	4.44	5.33	

	SE	DE	ML	RR	RD	RT	RQ
Ten entries							
Seeded position 1	3	4	3	9	6	7	
Seeded position 2	3	5	3	9	6	7	
Seeded position 3	2	5	3	9	6	8	
Seeded position 4	2	4	3	9	6	7	
Seeded position 5	1	4	3	9	4	7	
Seeded position 6	1	4	3	9	4	8	
Seeded position 7	2	3	3	9	4	2	
Seeded position 8	2	3	3	9	4	2	
Seeded position 9	1	2	3	9	4	3	
Seeded position 10	1	2	3	9	4	3	
Total	9.00	18.00	15.00	45.00	24.00	27.00	
Maximum	3.00	5.00	3.00	9.00	6.00	8.00	
Minimum	1.00	2.00	3.00	9.00	4.00	2.00	
Mean	1.80	3.60	3.00	9.00	4.80	5.40	
Eleven entries							
Seeded position 1	3	4	3	10	6	7	
Seeded position 2	3	5	3	10	7	8	
Seeded position 3	2	5	3	10	6	8	
Seeded position 4	2	4	4	10	7	7	
Seeded position 5	1	4	3	10	4	8	
Seeded position 6	2	5	3	10	5	8	
Seeded position 7	2	3	3	10	4	2	
Seeded position 8	2	4	3	10	5	3	
Seeded position 9	1	2	3	10	4	3	
Seeded position 10	1	2	3	10	5	3	
Seeded position 11	1	2	3	10	5	3	
Total	10.00	20.00	17.00	55.00	29.00	30.00	
Maximum	3.00	5.00	4.00	10.00	7.00	8.00	
Minimum	1.00	2.00	3.00	10.00	4.00	3.00	
Mean	1.82	3.64	3.09	10.00	5.27	5.45	
Twelve entries							
Seeded position 1	3	4	3	11	7	8	5
Seeded position 2	3	5	3	11	7	8	5
Seeded position 3	2	5	4	11	7	8	5
Seeded position 4	2	4	4	11	7	8	5
Seeded position 5	2	5	3	11	5	8	3
Seeded position 6	2	5	3	11	5	8	3
Seeded position 7	2	4	3	11	5	3	3
Seeded position 8	2	4	3	11	5	3	3
Seeded position 9	2	4	3	11	5	3	3
Seeded position 10	1	2	4	11	5	3	2
Seeded position 11	1	2	3	11	5	3	2
Seeded position 12	1	2	3	11	5	3	2
Total	11.00	22.00	20.00	66.00	34.00	23.00	20.00
Maximum	3.00	5.00	4.00	11.00	7.00	8.00	5.00
Minimum	1.00	2.00	3.00	11.00	5.00	3.00	2.00
Mean	1.43	3.67	3.33	11.00	5.67	3.50	3.33

(continued)

Table 1.3 *(continued)*

	SE	DE	ML	RR	RD	RT	RQ
Thirteen entries							
Seeded position 1	3	4	3	12	7	8	5
Seeded position 2	3	5	3	12	8	8	5
Seeded position 3	2	5	4	12	7	9	5
Seeded position 4	3	5	4	12	8	8	6
Seeded position 5	2	5	4	12	5	8	3
Seeded position 6	2	5	3	12	6	9	3
Seeded position 7	2	4	3	12	5	3	3
Seeded position 8	2	4	3	12	6	3	4
Seeded position 9	1	2	3	12	5	4	2
Seeded position 10	1	3	4	12	6	3	2
Seeded position 11	1	2	4	12	5	3	2
Seeded position 12	1	2	3	12	6	4	3
Seeded position 13	1	2	3	12	6	4	3
Total	12.00	24.00	22.00	78.00	40.00	37.00	23.00
Maximum	3.00	5.00	4.00	12.00	8.00	9.00	6.00
Minimum	1.00	2.00	3.00	12.00	5.00	3.00	2.00
Mean	1.85	3.69	3.38	12.00	6.15	5.69	3.34
Fourteen entries							
Seeded position 1	3	4	3	13	8	8	5
Seeded position 2	3	5	4	13	8	9	5
Seeded position 3	3	6	4	13	8	9	6
Seeded position 4	3	5	4	13	8	8	6
Seeded position 5	2	5	4	13	6	9	3
Seeded position 6	2	5	3	13	6	9	3
Seeded position 7	2	4	3	13	6	3	4
Seeded position 8	2	4	4	13	6	4	4
Seeded position 9	1	3	4	13	6	4	2
Seeded position 10	1	3	4	13	6	3	2
Seeded position 11	1	2	3	13	6	4	3
Seeded position 12	1	2	4	13	6	4	3
Seeded position 13	1	2	3	13	6	4	3
Seeded position 14	1	2	3	13	6	4	3
Total	13.00	26.00	25.00	91.00	46.00	41.00	26.00
Maximum	3.00	6.00	4.00	13.00	8.00	9.00	6.00
Minimum	1.00	2.00	3.00	13.00	6.00	3.00	2.00
Mean	1.86	3.71	3.57	13.00	6.57	5.86	3.71
Fifteen entries							
Seeded position 1	3	4	3	14	8	9	5
Seeded position 2	4	6	4	14	9	9	6
Seeded position 3	3	6	4	14	8	9	6
Seeded position 4	3	5	4	14	9	9	6
Seeded position 5	2	5	4	14	6	9	3
Seeded position 6	2	5	4	14	7	9	4
Seeded position 7	2	4	4	14	6	4	4

	SE	DE	ML	RR	RD	RT	RQ
Seeded position 8	2	4	4	14	7	4	4
Seeded position 9	1	3	4	14	6	4	2
Seeded position 10	1	3	4	14	7	4	3
Seeded position 11	1	2	3	14	6	4	3
Seeded position 12	1	3	4	14	7	4	3
Seeded position 13	1	2	3	14	6	4	3
Seeded position 14	1	2	4	14	7	4	3
Seeded position 15	1	2	3	14	7	4	3
Total	14.00	28.00	28.00	105.00	53.00	45.00	29.00
Maximum	4.00	6.00	4.00	14.00	9.00	9.00	6.00
Minimum	1.00	2.00	3.00	14.00	6.00	4.00	3.00
Mean	1.88	3.73	3.73	14.00	7.07	6.00	3.87
Sixteen entries							
Seeded position 1	4	5	4	15	9	9	6
Seeded position 2	4	6	4	15	9	9	6
Seeded position 3	3	6	4	15	9	10	6
Seeded position 4	3	5	4	15	9	9	6
Seeded position 5	2	5	4	15	7	9	4
Seeded position 6	2	5	4	15	7	10	4
Seeded position 7	2	4	4	15	7	4	4
Seeded position 8	2	4	4	15	7	4	4
Seeded position 9	1	3	4	15	7	5	3
Seeded position 10	1	3	4	15	7	4	3
Seeded position 11	1	3	4	15	7	4	3
Seeded position 12	1	3	4	15	7	5	3
Seeded position 13	1	2	4	15	7	4	3
Seeded position 14	1	2	4	15	7	4	3
Seeded position 15	1	2	4	15	7	5	3
Seeded position 16	1	2	4	15	7	5	3
Total	15.00	30.00	32.00	120.00	60.00	50.00	32.00
Maximum	4.00	6.00	4.00	15.00	9.00	10.00	6.00
Minimum	1.00	2.00	4.00	15.00	7.00	4.00	3.00
Mean	1.88	3.75	4.00	15.00	7.50	6.25	4.00

round robin-triple split (RT) was calculated assuming a six-person round robin (RR) play-off for the top two finishers in each of the three pools. The round robin-quadruple split (RQ) was calculated assuming a single-elimination (SE), eight-entry play-off with a third- and fourth-place match. The SE and RR do not have any additional play-off structure. The equitable seeding was used.

The following example illustrates how you can use the tables. If there were 12 entries and sufficient time, the RR would clearly be the best for equalizing the number of games played, because in the RR everyone plays the same number of games. However, the RR would require 66 games. If you want to limit the number of games, then the multilevel (ML) tournament would be the next best choice. The total number of games is decreased from 66 to 20, and the difference between the number of games played is only one, with the maximum games played equaling four and minimum played equaling three. However, one difficulty of the ML tournament is that it does not allow players who lost a match to regain their position, something that the round robin-split tournament and the DE do. Of those tournament types, you would be likely to prefer the RD because the spread in the number of games played is only two, with a maximum of seven games to a minimum of five. However, this format would require 34 games. If 34 games are too many, then the other three options are available. However, you can quickly dismiss the RT because it requires only one game less and significantly increases the spread in number of games played. For the remaining two formats, the DE is slightly better than the RQ in equalizing the number of games played, but the RQ requires two fewer games. Finally, if you want the fewest number of games and are not concerned that this choice would mean a format with the highest relative spread in the number of games played per entry, then the SE would be the choice. The SE requires only 11 games, but those playing in the maximum number of games play in three times as many games as those who play only one game in the entire tournament. This is one of the worst formats for equalizing the number of games per entries.

In addition to understanding the overall effects by looking at the total, maximum, minimum, and mean number of games played, it is also important to see who is most affected by limiting the number of games. For 12 entries, RT, SE, RQ, and DE disadvantage the low-seeded players by eliminating them early from the tournament. The RT is the most unequal, and the DE is the best of these four alternatives. The RD and ML improve the number of games in which lower seeds participate. Obviously, the RR best equalizes the number of games played because each entry plays all others.

Though equalizing the number of games is most desirable in many tournament settings, the reality of time and facility constraints often impose adjustments to this goal. With Table 1.3, the tournament director will know the effect different tournament options have on the number of games each entry participates in.

Here is a list of the order in which the seeds were placed on the sample draw sheet, according to their starting positions, with starting positions labeled A through H:

Starting position	Entry
A	SEED 1
B	BYE
C	SEED 3
D	BYE
E	SEED 5
F	SEED 4
G	BYE
H	SEED 2

To make your work easier and reduce errors, each of the following chapters provides you with draw sheets as well as seeding charts. The seeding chart below is basically the same as this position list, except that it provides seeding for up to 16 entries. Also, the word "Seed" has been deleted and the word "Bye" is replaced by the letter *B*.

As tournament director you should rank the entries according to the information you have available; then enter them onto the appropriate draw sheet as recommended by the seeding table. There may be upsets, but at least you can be assured that you have done your best to ensure a good tournament.

Byes

A bye occurs when there are fewer players than spaces on the tournament draw, and the top-ranked players do not play anyone in the first round. In

Equitable Seeding for Single- and Double-Elimination Tournaments

Starting position	Number of entries													
	3	4	5	6	7	8	9	10	11	12	13	14	15	16
A	1	1	1	1	1	1	1	1	1	1	1	1	1	1
B	B	3	B	B	B	7	B	B	B	B	B	B	B	11
C	3	4	B	6	6	6	B	10	10	10	10	10	10	10
D	2	2	3	3	3	3	7	7	7	7	7	7	7	7
E			4	4	4	4	6	6	6	6	6	6	6	6
F			5	5	5	5	B	B	11	12	13	14	15	16
G			B	B	7	8	B	B	B	B	B	11	12	13
H			2	2	2	2	3	3	3	3	3	3	3	3
I							4	4	4	4	4	4	4	4
J							B	B	B	B	11	12	13	14
K							B	B	B	11	12	13	14	15
L							5	5	5	5	5	5	5	5
M							8	8	8	8	8	8	8	8
N							9	9	9	9	9	9	9	9
O							B	B	B	B	B	B	11	12
P							2	2	2	2	2	2	2	2

figure 1.1, the top-ranked entries do not play anyone in the first round but automatically advance to the second round; they all receive a bye. Meanwhile the fourth- and fifth-seeded entries play each other to see which one will advance to the second round.

Using the Draw Sheets

Before we look at the individual tournaments, it will be helpful to briefly explain the numbers used in figure 1.1 and the example below. The numbers on the draw sheet indicate the game numbers. In other words, game number 1 involves seed 4 playing seed 5; games number 2 involves seed 1 playing seed 3, and so on. The playing schedule in the example below indicates which games should be played when. Games 1 and 2 could be played first, followed by 3, and concluding with game 4. We also list an alternative schedule, which provides a shorter break for the winner of game 2 before the final match. The letters PA stand for playing area. Schedules for the relevant number of playing areas are provided, and the appropriate one should be selected.

Playing schedule						

Five entries

Two playing areas

PA I	1	3	4	or	1	2	4
PA II	2					3	

Once you have decided which tournament to use, you will notice how easy it is to assign entries to a draw sheet and schedule your competition. You are on your way to implementing a successful tournament.

CHAPTER 2

Single-Elimination Tournament

Advantages	Disadvantages
• The format is easy to understand.	• Each entrant is guaranteed only one game.
• It accommodates a large number of entries.	• Accurate seeding is crucial.
• It requires few games.	• It does not maximize the use of multiple playing areas.
• It requires few playing areas.	

Best use: Playoff games at season's end or following a long tournament.

■ Implementing the single elimination is straightforward. Once you have seeded players, you can enter them on the draw sheets as suggested by the seeding tables. Then, select the appropriate schedule, and play can get under way. Place the name of each player who wins on the draw sheet to the right of that player's previously recorded game. Eliminate those who lose.

One option to consider for ending a single elimination tournament is to have the semifinal losers play each other. This consolation or third-place match provides opportunity for establishing the third- and fourth-place positions and may also offer the first- and second-place teams a one-game break before playing their championship match.

The procedure for large, single-elimination tournaments is the same as for small ones. If you have more than 16 entries, for example, 32 entries, it would be best to seed them into four single elimination draw sheets of eight entries each. The winner of these draws would be placed in a predetermined manner on a final draw sheet of four entries. If you had 64 entries you might select four draw sheets of 16 or eight draw sheets of eight, with the winner going to a final draw sheet of either four or eight respectively. For other options on dealing with a large number of entries, see chapter 7.

The method of determining the number of games is this:

Number of entries − 1 = number of games

Starting position	Number of entries													
	3	**4**	**5**	**6**	**7**	**8**	**9**	**10**	**11**	**12**	**13**	**14**	**15**	**16**
A	1	1	1	1	1	1	1	1	1	1	1	1	1	1
B	B	3	B	B	B	7	B	B	B	B	B	B	B	11
C	3	4	B	6	6	6	B	10	10	10	10	10	10	10
D	2	2	3	3	3	3	7	7	7	7	7	7	7	7
E			4	4	4	4	6	6	6	6	6	6	6	6
F			5	5	5	5	B	B	11	12	13	14	15	16
G			B	B	7	8	B	B	B	B	B	11	12	13
H			2	2	2	2	3	3	3	3	3	3	3	3
I							4	4	4	4	4	4	4	4
J							B	B	B	B	11	12	13	14
K							B	B	B	11	12	13	14	15
L							5	5	5	5	5	5	5	5
M							8	8	8	8	8	8	8	8
N							9	9	9	9	9	9	9	9
O							B	B	B	B	B	B	11	12
P							2	2	2	2	2	2	2	2

Table title: **Equitable Seeding For Single- and Double-Elimination Tournaments**

Advantage Seeding For Single- and Double-Elimination Tournaments

Starting position	Number of entries													
	3	4	5	6	7	8	9	10	11	12	13	14	15	16
A	1	1	1	1	1	1	1	1	1	1	1	1	1	1
B	B	4	B	B	B	8	B	B	B	B	B	B	B	16
C	3	3	5	5	5	5	9	9	9	9	9	9	9	9
D	2	2	4	4	4	4	8	8	8	8	8	8	8	8
E			3	3	3	3	5	5	5	5	5	5	5	5
F			B	6	6	6	B	B	B	12	12	12	12	12
G			B	B	7	7	B	B	B	B	13	13	13	13
H			2	2	2	2	4	4	4	4	4	4	4	4
I							3	3	3	3	3	3	3	3
J							B	B	B	B	B	14	14	14
K							B	B	11	11	11	11	11	11
L							6	6	6	6	6	6	6	6
M							7	7	7	7	7	7	7	7
N							B	10	10	10	10	10	10	10
O							B	B	B	B	B	B	15	15
P							2	2	2	2	2	2	2	2

Single-elimination tournament with three entries

Tournament _____   **Date** _____

Round   1   2

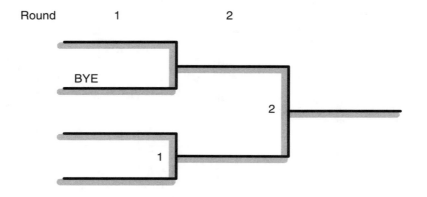

BYE

From Organizing Successful Tournaments, 2nd ed. by John Byl, 1999, Champaign, IL: Human Kinetics. Copyright 1999 by John Byl.

Single-elimination tournament with four entries

Tournament _____ **Date** _____

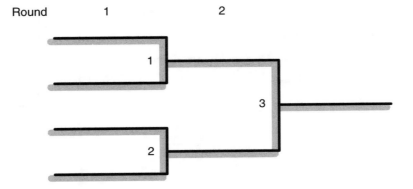

Round   1   2

From Organizing Successful Tournaments, 2nd ed. by John Byl, 1999, Champaign, IL: Human Kinetics. Copyright 1999 by John Byl.

Single-elimination tournament with five entries

Tournament _____   **Date** _____

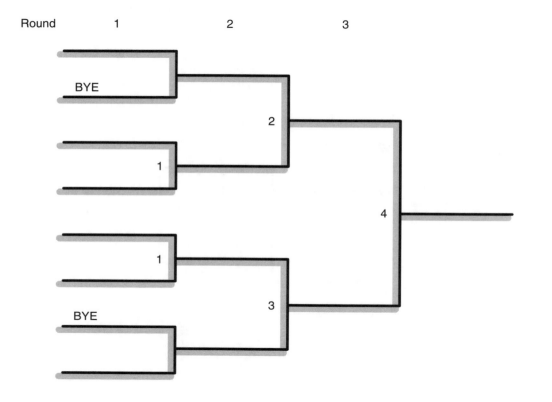

Round   1   2   3

BYE

1

2

1

BYE

3

4

From Organizing Successful Tournaments, 2nd ed. by John Byl, 1999, Champaign, IL: Human Kinetics. Copyright 1999 by John Byl.

Single-elimination tournament with six entries

Tournament _____   **Date** _____

Round   1   2   3

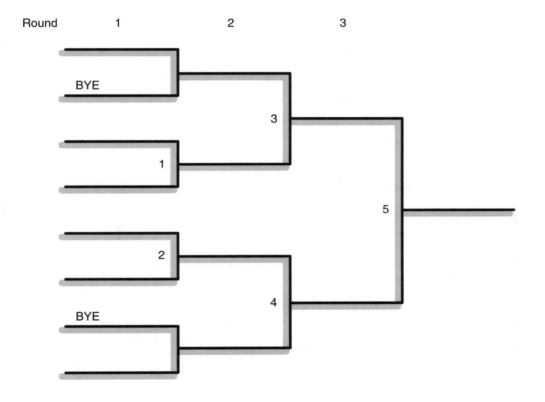

From Organizing Successful Tournaments, 2nd ed. by John Byl, 1999, Champaign, IL: Human Kinetics. Copyright 1999 by John Byl.

Tournament _____ **Date** _____

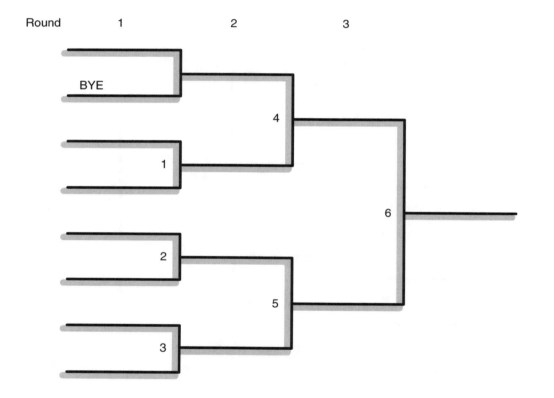

Round   1   2   3

BYE

From Organizing Successful Tournaments, 2nd ed. by John Byl, 1999, Champaign, IL: Human Kinetics. Copyright 1999 by John Byl.

Single-elimination tournament with eight entries

Tournament _____ **Date** _____

Round   1   2   3

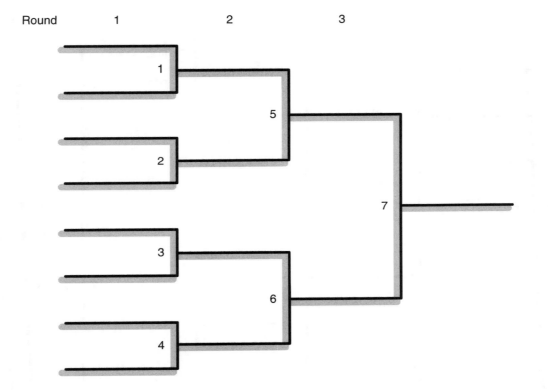

From Organizing Successful Tournaments, 2nd ed. by John Byl, 1999, Champaign, IL: Human Kinetics. Copyright 1999 by John Byl.

Single-elimination tournament with nine entries

Tournament _____ **Date** _____

Round   1   2   3   4

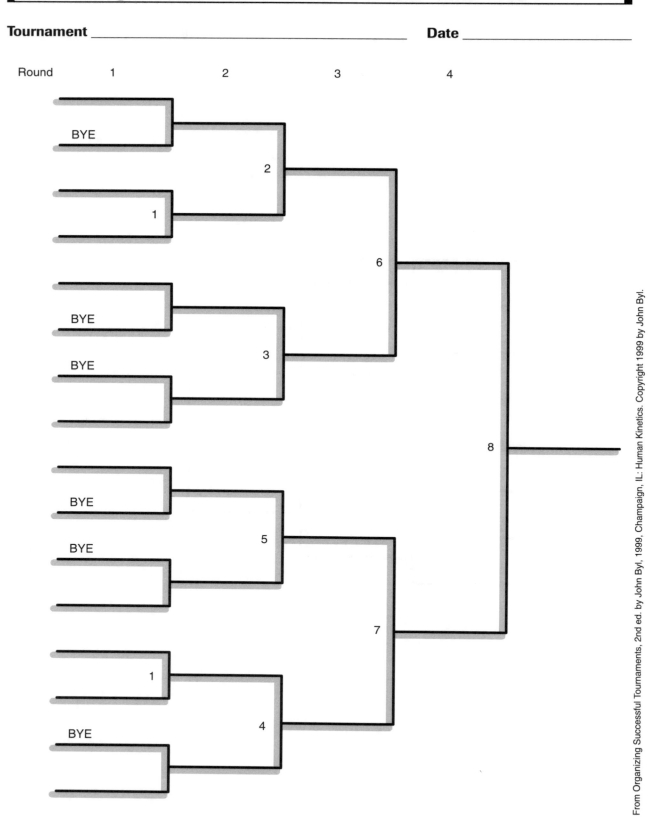

From Organizing Successful Tournaments, 2nd ed. by John Byl, 1999, Champaign, IL: Human Kinetics. Copyright 1999 by John Byl.

Single-elimination tournament with 10 entries

Tournament _____   **Date** _____

Round   1   2   3   4

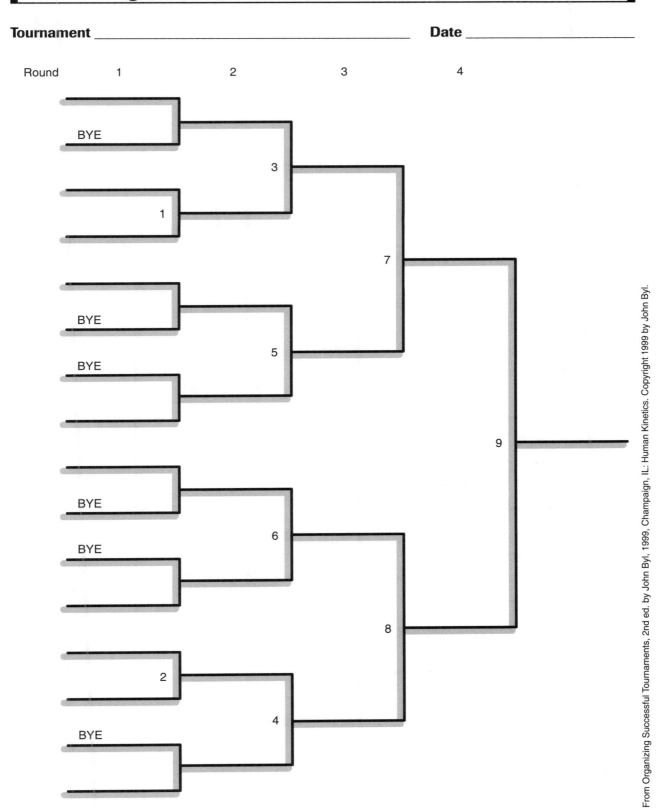

From Organizing Successful Tournaments, 2nd ed. by John Byl, 1999, Champaign, IL: Human Kinetics. Copyright 1999 by John Byl.

Single-elimination tournament with 11 entries

Tournament _____ **Date** _____

Round   1   2   3   4

From Organizing Successful Tournaments, 2nd ed. by John Byl, 1999, Champaign, IL: Human Kinetics. Copyright 1999 by John Byl.

Single-elimination tournament with 12 entries

Tournament _____ **Date** _____

Round   1   2   3   4

From Organizing Successful Tournaments, 2nd ed. by John Byl, 1999, Champaign, IL: Human Kinetics. Copyright 1999 by John Byl.

Single-elimination tournament with 13 entries

Tournament _____ Date _____

Round   1   2   3   4

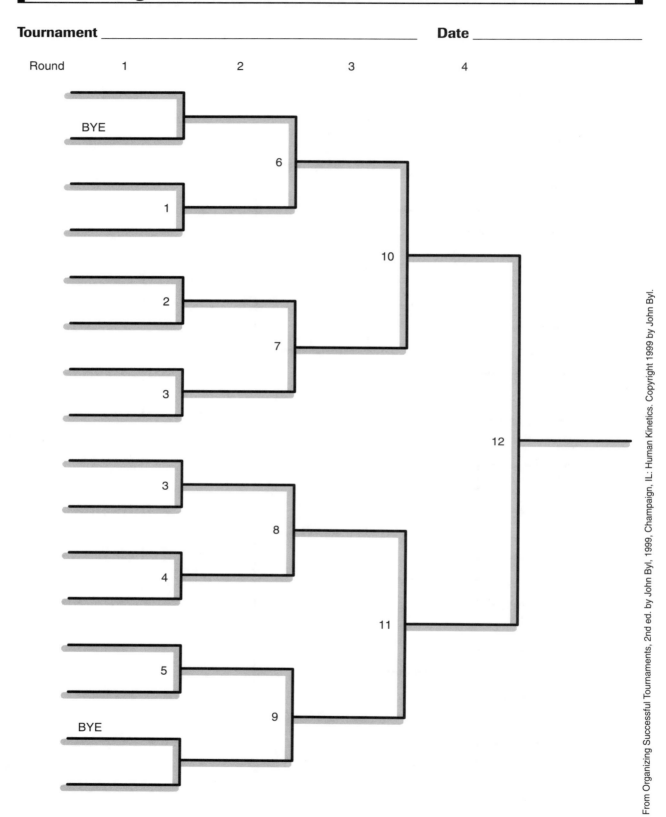

From Organizing Successful Tournaments, 2nd ed. by John Byl, 1999, Champaign, IL: Human Kinetics. Copyright 1999 by John Byl.

Single-elimination tournament with 14 entries

Round   1   2   3   4

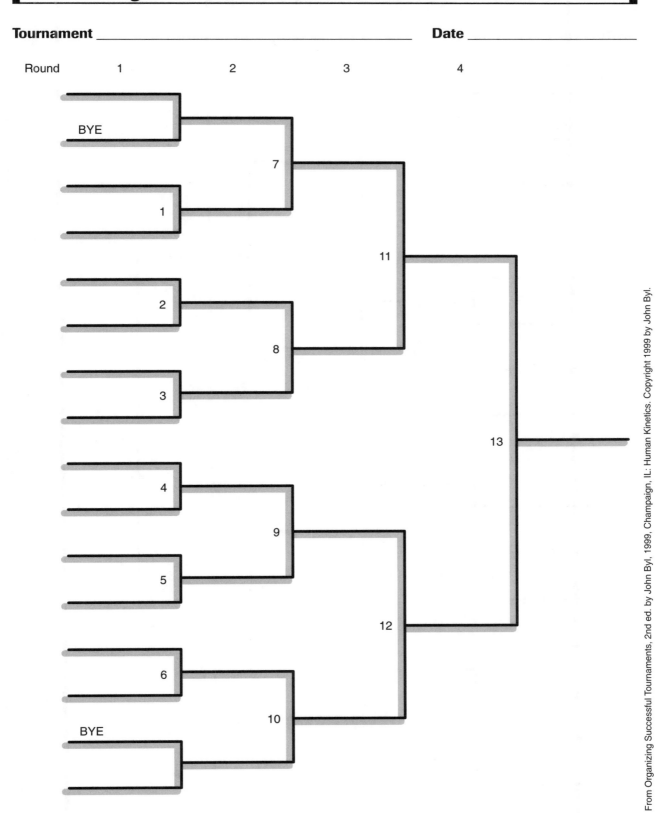

From Organizing Successful Tournaments, 2nd ed. by John Byl, 1999, Champaign, IL: Human Kinetics. Copyright 1999 by John Byl.

Single-elimination tournament with 15 entries

Tournament _____ **Date** _____

Round   1   2   3   4

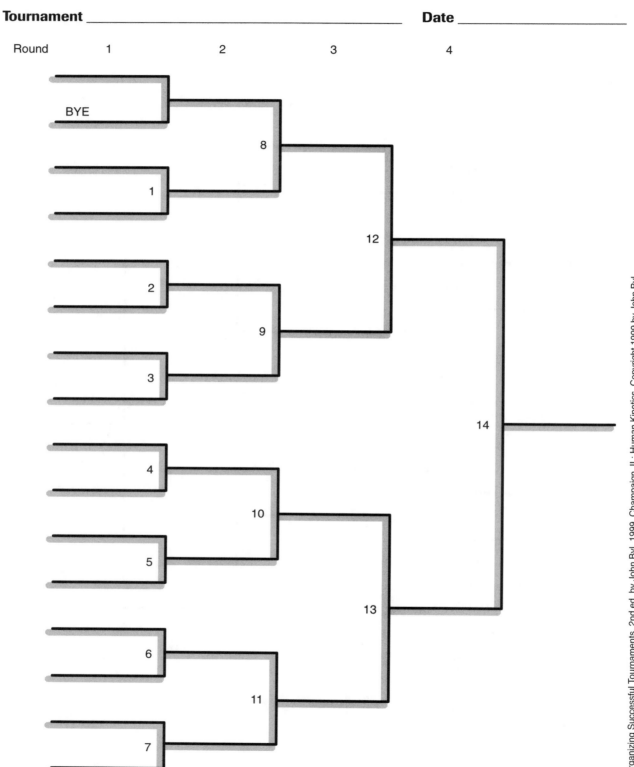

From Organizing Successful Tournaments, 2nd ed. by John Byl, 1999, Champaign, IL: Human Kinetics. Copyright 1999 by John Byl.

Single-elimination tournament with 16 entries

Tournament _____ **Date** _____

Round   1   2   3   4

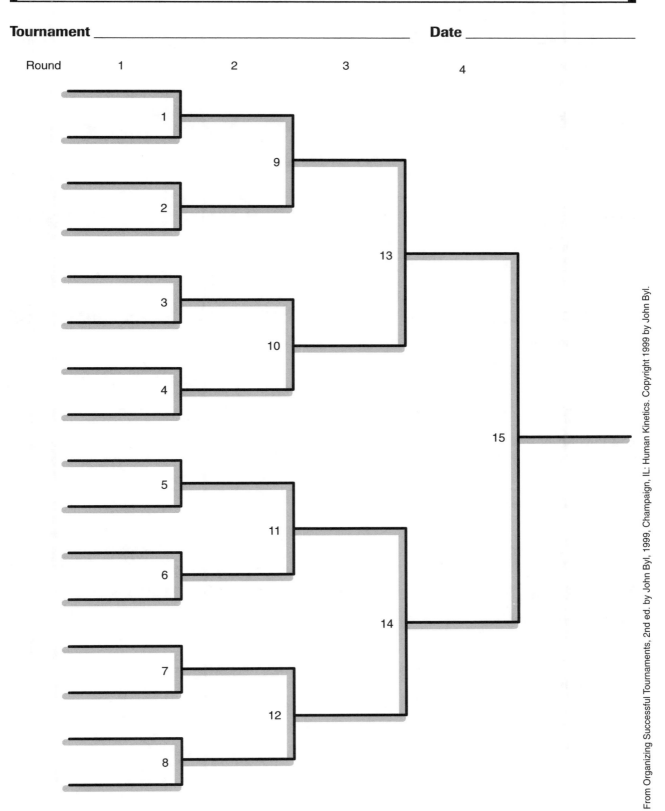

From Organizing Successful Tournaments, 2nd ed. by John Byl, 1999, Champaign, IL: Human Kinetics. Copyright 1999 by John Byl.

PLAYING SCHEDULES

THREE ENTRIES

One Playing Area

PA I	1	2

FOUR ENTRIES

Two Playing Areas

PA I	1	3
PA II	2	

FIVE ENTRIES

Two Playing Areas

PA I	1	3	4	or	1	2	4
PA II	2					3	

SIX ENTRIES

Two Playing Areas

PA I	1	3	5
PA II	2	4	

SEVEN ENTRIES

Two Playing Areas

PA I	1	3	5	6	or	1	2	4	6
PA II	2	4					3	5	

Three Playing Areas

PA I	1	5	6
PA II	2	4	
PA III	3		

EIGHT ENTRIES

Two Playing Areas

PA I	1	3	6	7
PA II	2	4	5	

Three Playing Areas

PA I	1	4	6	7	or	1	3	5	7
PA II	2	5				2	4	6	
PA III	3								

PLAYING SCHEDULES

Four Playing Areas

PA I	1	6	7
PA II	2	5	
PA III	3		
PA IV	4		

NINE ENTRIES

Two Playing Areas

PA I	1	3	5	7	8
PA II	2	4		6	

Three Playing Areas

PA I	1	6	7	8	or	1	4	7	8
PA II	2	5				2	5	6	
PA III	3	4				3			

Four Playing Areas

PA I	1	5	7	8	or	1	4	7	8
PA II	2	6				2	5	6	
PA III	3					3			
PA IV	4								

10 ENTRIES

Three Playing Areas

PA I	1	4	7	9
PA II	2	5	8
PA III	3	6	

Four Playing Areas

PA I	1	6	7	9	or	1	3	7	9
PA II	2	5	8			2	4	8	
PA III	3					5			
PA IV	4					6			

11 ENTRIES

Three Playing Areas

PA I	1	4	7	9	10	or	4	6	8	10
PA II	2	5	8				5	7	9	
PA III	3	6								

Four Playing Areas

PA I	1	5	9	10
PA II	2	6	8	
PA III	3	7		
PA IV	4			

(continued)

PLAYING SCHEDULES

12 ENTRIES

Three Playing Areas

PA I	1	4	7	9	11
PA II	2	5	8	10	
PA III	3	6			

Four Playing Areas

PA I	1	8	9	11
PA II	2	7	10	
PA III	3	6		
PA IV	4	5		

13 ENTRIES

Three Playing Areas

PA I	1	4	7	11	12
PA II	2	5	8	10	
PA III	3	6	9		

Four Playing Areas

PA I	1	5	9	11	12	or	5	8	10	12
PA II	2	8	10				6	9	11
PA III	3	6					7		
PA IV	4	7							

Five Playing Areas

PA I	1	8	10	12
PA II	2	9	11	
PA III	3	6		
PA IV	4	7		
PA V	5			

14 ENTRIES

Three Playing Areas

PA I	1	4	7	10	12	13	or	7	9	11	13
PA II	2	5	8	11				8	10	12
PA III	3	6	9						

Four Playing Areas

PA I	1	5	9	12	13	or	9	11	13
PA II	2	6	10				10	12	
PA III	3	7	11						
PA IV	4	8							

PLAYING SCHEDULES

Five Playing Areas

PA I	1	6	9	12	13	or	9	11	13
PA II	2	7	10				10	12
PA III	3	8	11
PA IV	4
PA V	5

15 ENTRIES

Three Playing Areas

PA I	1	4	7	10	13	14	or	10	12	14
PA II	2	5	8					11	13
PA III	3	6	9	12

Four Playing Areas

PA I	1	5	9	12	14
PA II	2	6	10	13
PA III	3	7	11
PA IV	4	8

Five Playing Areas

PA I	1	6	10	13	14	or	10	12	14
PA II	2	7	11				11	13
PA III	3	8	12
PA IV	4	9
PA V	5

Six Playing Areas

PA I	1	7	11	13	14	or	7	10	12	14
PA II	2	8	12				8	11	13
PA III	3	9					9
PA IV	4	10
PA V	5
PA VI	6

Seven Playing Areas

PA I	1	11	12	14
PA II	2	10	13
PA III	3	9
PA IV	4	8
PA V	5
PA VI	6
PA VII	7

(continued)

PLANNING SCHEDULES

16 ENTRIES

Three Playing Areas

PA I	1	4	7	10	13	15
PA II	2	5	8	11	14	
PA III	3	6	9	12		

Four Playing Areas

PA I	1	5	12	13	15
PA II	2	6	11	14	
PA III	3	7	10		
PA IV	4	8	9		

Five Playing Areas

PA I	1	6	11	14	15	or	11	13	15
PA II	2	7	12				12	14	
PA III	3	8	13						
PA IV	4	9							
PA V	5	10							

Six Playing Areas

PA I	1	7	11	14	15	or	11	13	15
PA II	2	8	12				12	14	
PA III	3	9	13						
PA IV	4	10							
PA V	5								
PA VI	6								

Seven Playing Areas

PA I	1	8	12	14	15
PA II	2	9	13		
PA III	3	10			
PA IV	4	11			
PA V	5				
PA VI	6				
PA VII	7				

Eight Playing Areas

PA I	1	12	13	15
PA II	2	11	14	
PA III	3	10		
PA IV	4	9		
PA V	5			
PA VI	6			
PA VII	7			
PA VIII	8			

CHAPTER 3

Multilevel Tournament

Advantages	Disadvantages
• All entrants play about the same number of games.	• First-round losers rank in the bottom half of entries.
• There are few lopsided games.	• Accurate seeding is crucial.
• It requires few games.	
• It uses multiple playing areas efficiently.	
• Each entrant has more games than in single or double elimination.	

Best use: For classes and intramural and recreational settings
in which eliminating entrants is undesirable and final standings aren't crucial

■ We can best understand the multilevel tournament as a single-elimination tournament with many consolation rounds. The intent of the multilevel format is threefold: to avoid eliminating participants who lose, to provide as many closely contested games as possible, and to do this within a reasonable time limit. We have provided a seeding table and draw sheets to assist you.

It is perhaps best to explain this tournament by taking you through an example of a multilevel, eight-entry tournament as shown in figure 3.1. The top bracket is much the same as in a single-elimination tournament, seeding players according to the seeding chart and placing the name of each winning player on the line to the right of that player's previous game. The entry who goes to the far right without losing comes in first in section A and, therefore, first overall. The entry who was defeated last by the first-place entry would be in second place. However, unlike single elimination, in which half the entries for the tournament are eliminated following the first round of play, those who lose in the first round drop to section C and play in round two at that level. With respect to the goals of this tournament type, those who lose continue to play, and all entries will be playing someone close to their ability level in this round. Following the second round, those who lost in section A now drop to section B, and those who lost in section C now drop to section D. Once again, no entry is eliminated from the tournament, and all entries play someone close in ability in the final round.

The strengths of this tournament are obvious. First, all entries play the same number of games. Second, the similarity in the level of play is close in round two and even closer in round three; in other words, each round sees entries playing others of more similar ability—which often creates the most satisfying games. The multilevel tournament takes less time than double elimination because it requires fewer games. Considering these three strengths, this is a tournament well worth using. However, as in single elimination, precise seeding is important. In the case illustrated in figure 3.1, those who lose in the first round can do no better than fifth overall; this is the major weakness of the multilevel tournament. Considering these strengths and weaknesses, you can see why this tournament is well suited to physical education classes or intramural settings where equality of playing time is important.

For a multilevel tournament involving more than 16 entries, there are two possible solutions. The first is to divide the entries into two pools, each playing in a multilevel format, then have a play-off for the A-level players or the A- and B-level players. A second option, one that is more time consuming, is to prepare one multilevel tournament including all the entries. To limit the length of play, limit the levels to four (note that this changes the number of games per entry). Limiting the levels to four ensures all entries of participating in at least three games. You could prepare level A using the single-elimination draw sheets and seeding tables in chapter 2. Those who lose in the first round would play in level C, a single-elimination draw suitable for a group half the size of level A. Those who lose in the second round would drop one level: Those in level A drop to level B, those in C drop to D. In the third and subsequent rounds a player would be eliminated from further play following a loss. You could draw the B to D levels using single-elimination draw sheets as well.

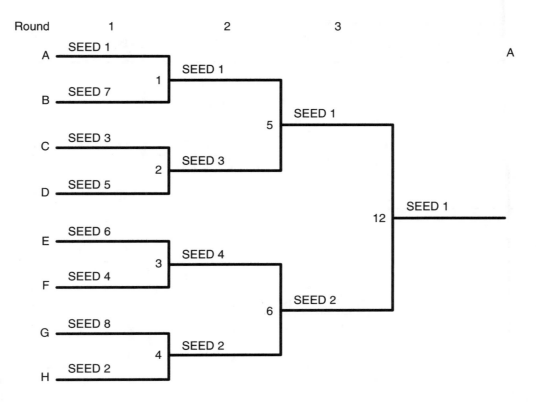

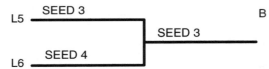

Figure 3.1 Multilevel tournament with eight entries.

Seeding For Multilevel Tournaments

Starting position	Number of entries										
	6	7	8	9	10	11	12	13	14	15	16
A	1	1	1	1	1	1	1	1	1	1	1
B	B	B	7	B	B	B	B	B	B	B	11
C	5	5	3	5	5	5	9	5	11	5	5
D	3	3	5	7	7	7	B	13	B	11	15
E	4	6	6	3	3	3	3	3	3	3	3
F	6	4	4	B	B	B	11	11	13	13	13
G	B	7	8	9	9	11	5	7	5	7	7
H	2	2	2	B	B	B	7	9	9	9	9
I				B	B	6	8	8	8	10	10
J				6	10	8	6	6	7	8	8
K				B	B	4	12	12	12	14	14
L				4	4	10	4	4	4	4	4
M				B	8	B	B	B	14	15	16
N				8	6	9	10	10	6	6	6
O				B	B	B	B	B	10	12	12
P				2	2	2	2	2	2	2	2

Multilevel tournament with six entries

Tournament _____   **Date** _____

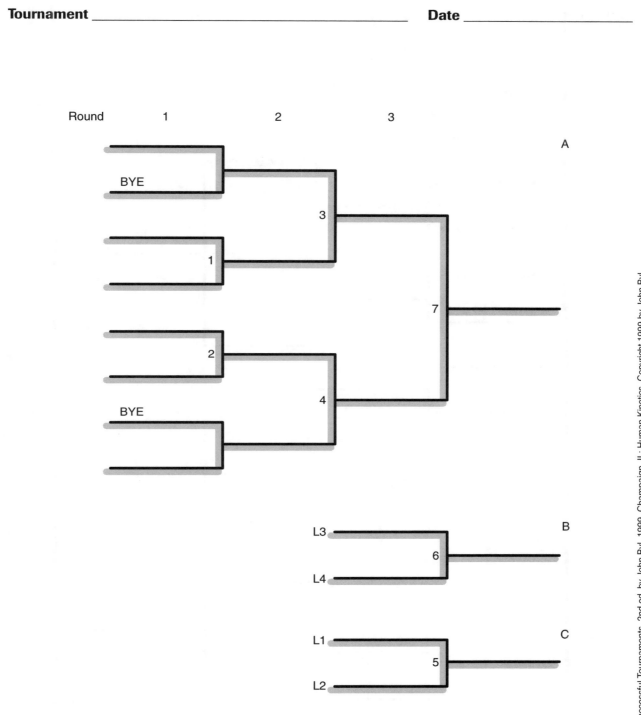

Round   1   2   3

From Organizing Successful Tournaments, 2nd ed. by John Byl, 1999, Champaign, IL: Human Kinetics. Copyright 1999 by John Byl.

Multilevel tournament with seven entries

Tournament _____ **Date** _____

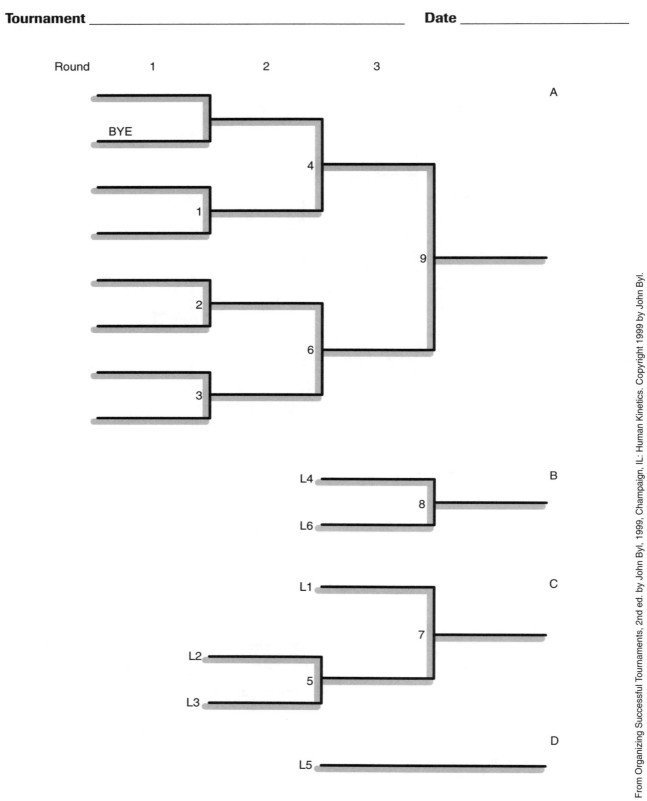

Round   1   2   3

From Organizing Successful Tournaments, 2nd ed. by John Byl, 1999, Champaign, IL: Human Kinetics. Copyright 1999 by John Byl.

Multilevel tournament with eight entries

Tournament _____ **Date** _____

Round   1   2   3

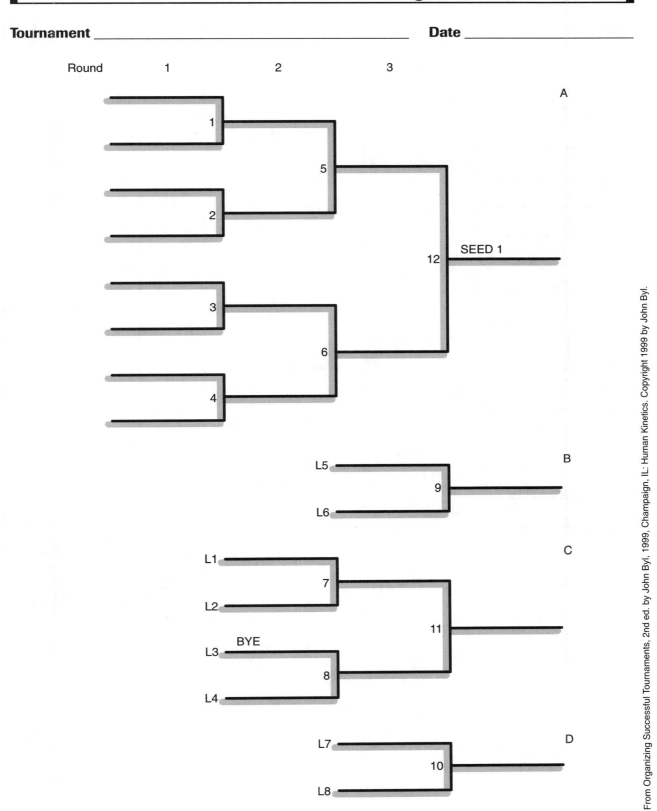

From Organizing Successful Tournaments, 2nd ed. by John Byl, 1999, Champaign, IL: Human Kinetics. Copyright 1999 by John Byl.

Multilevel tournament with nine entries

Tournament _____ **Date** _____

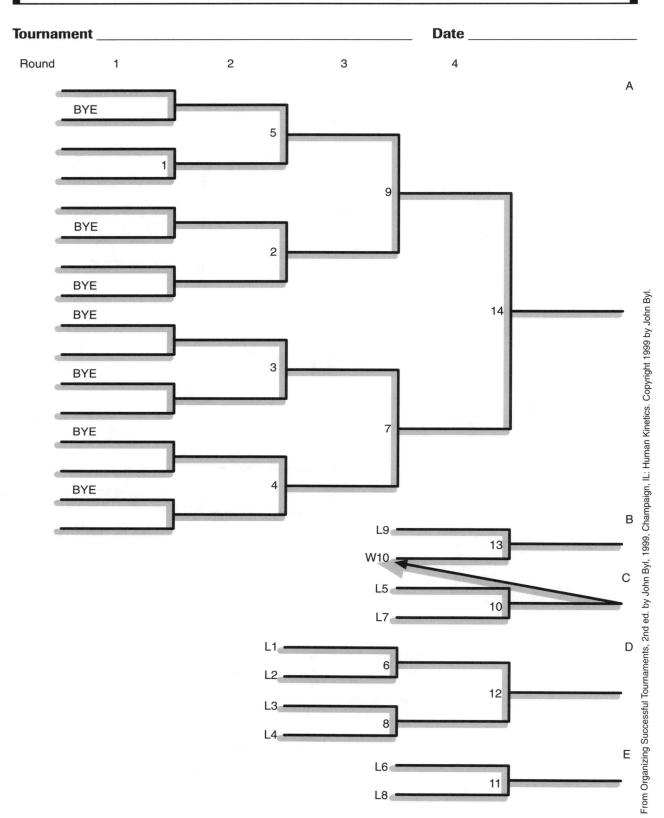

Round   1   2   3   4

From Organizing Successful Tournaments, 2nd ed. by John Byl, 1999, Champaign, IL: Human Kinetics. Copyright 1999 by John Byl.

Multilevel tournament with 10 entries

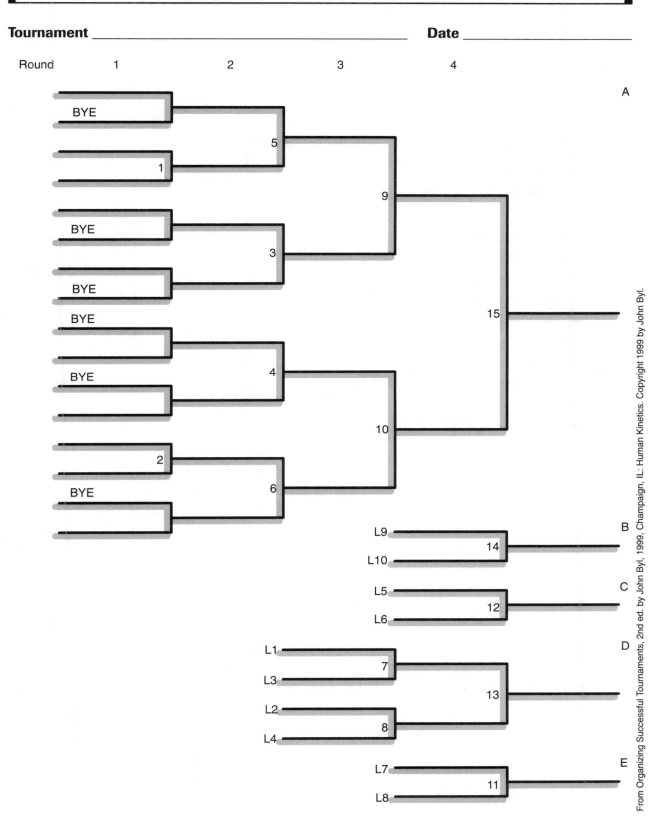

From Organizing Successful Tournaments, 2nd ed. by John Byl, 1999, Champaign, IL: Human Kinetics. Copyright 1999 by John Byl.

Multilevel tournament with 11 entries

Tournament _____ **Date** _____

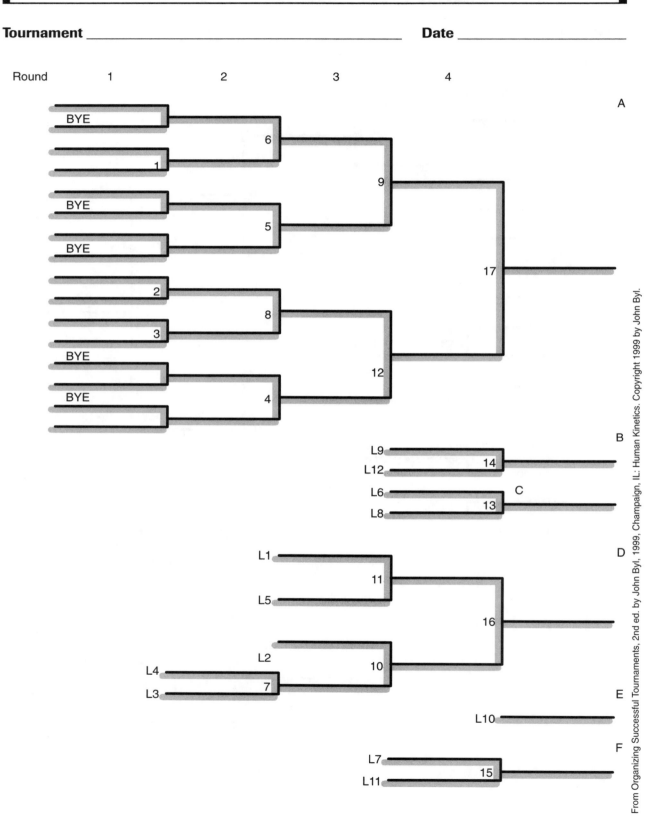

Round   1   2   3   4

From Organizing Successful Tournaments, 2nd ed. by John Byl, 1999, Champaign, IL: Human Kinetics. Copyright 1999 by John Byl.

Multilevel tournament with 12 entries

Tournament _____ **Date** _____

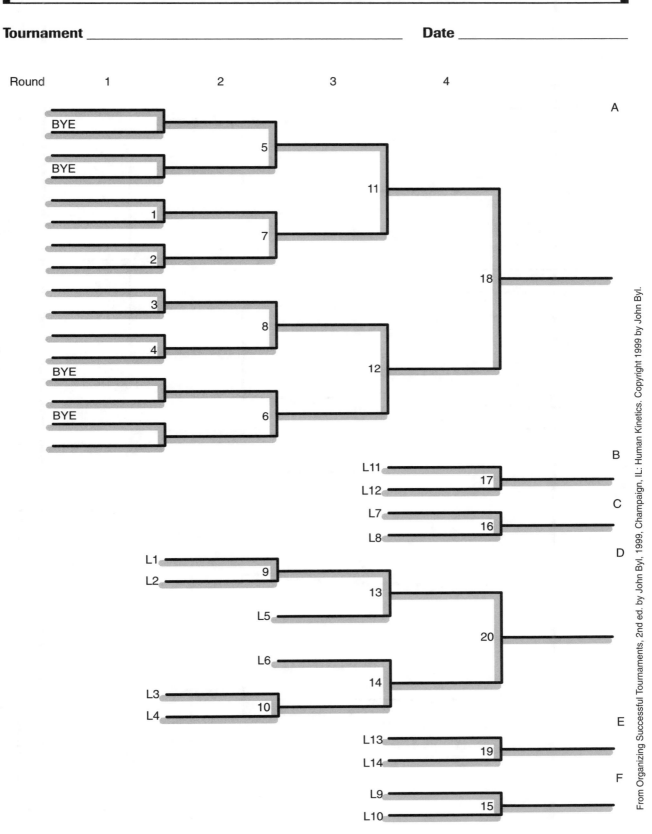

Round   1   2   3   4

From Organizing Successful Tournaments, 2nd ed. by John Byl, 1999, Champaign, IL: Human Kinetics. Copyright 1999 by John Byl.

Multilevel tournament with 13 entries

Tournament _____ Date _____

Round   1   2   3   4

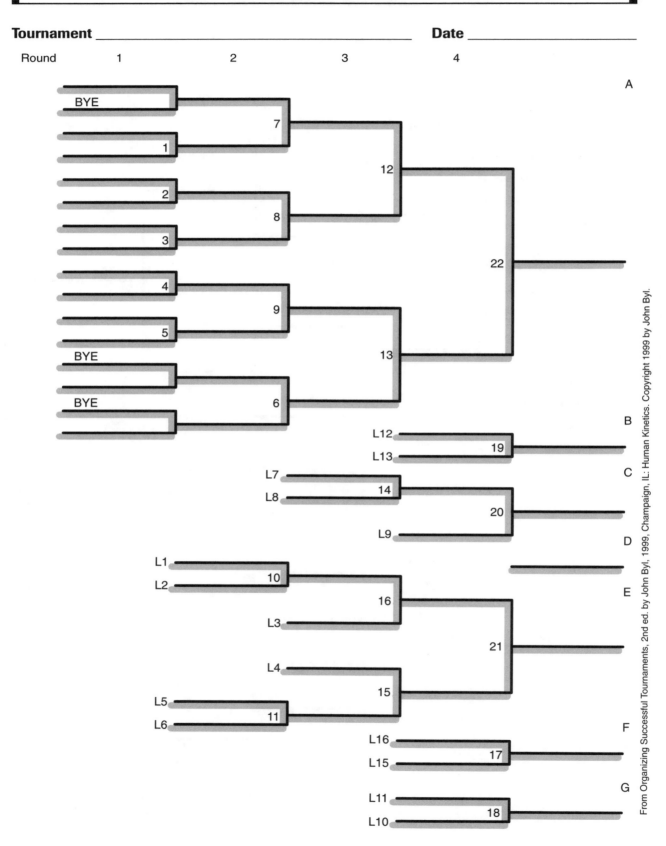

From Organizing Successful Tournaments, 2nd ed. by John Byl, 1999, Champaign, IL: Human Kinetics. Copyright 1999 by John Byl.

Multilevel tournament with 14 entries

Tournament _____ **Date** _____

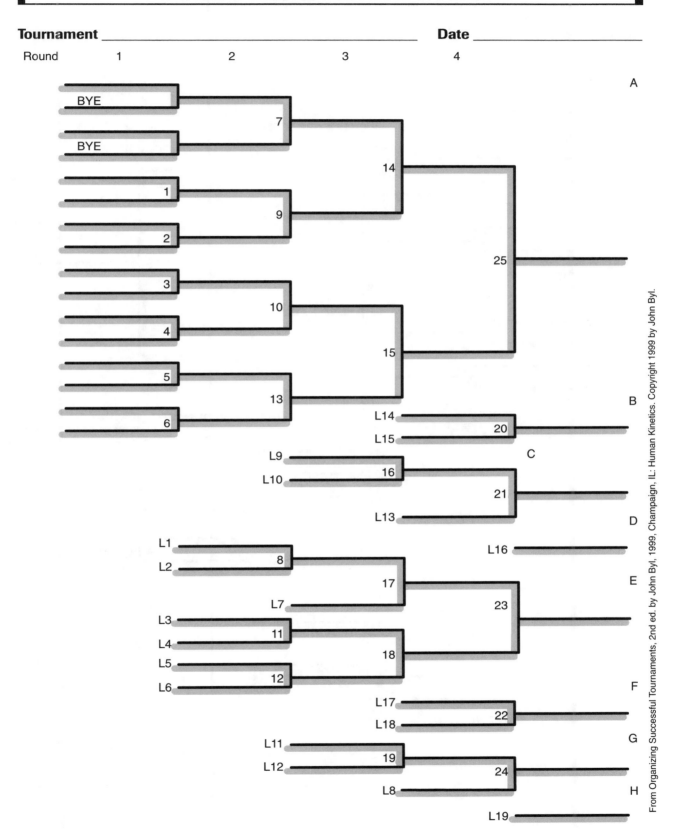

From Organizing Successful Tournaments, 2nd ed. by John Byl, 1999, Champaign, IL: Human Kinetics. Copyright 1999 by John Byl.

Multilevel tournament with 15 entries

Tournament _____ Date _____

Round   1   2   3   4

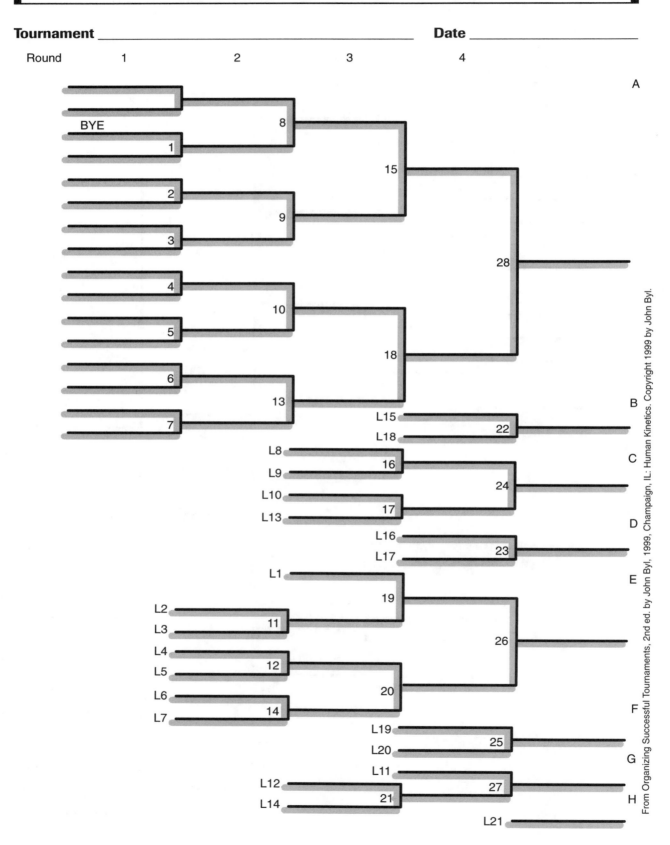

From Organizing Successful Tournaments, 2nd ed. by John Byl, 1999, Champaign, IL: Human Kinetics. Copyright 1999 by John Byl.

Multilevel tournament with 16 entries

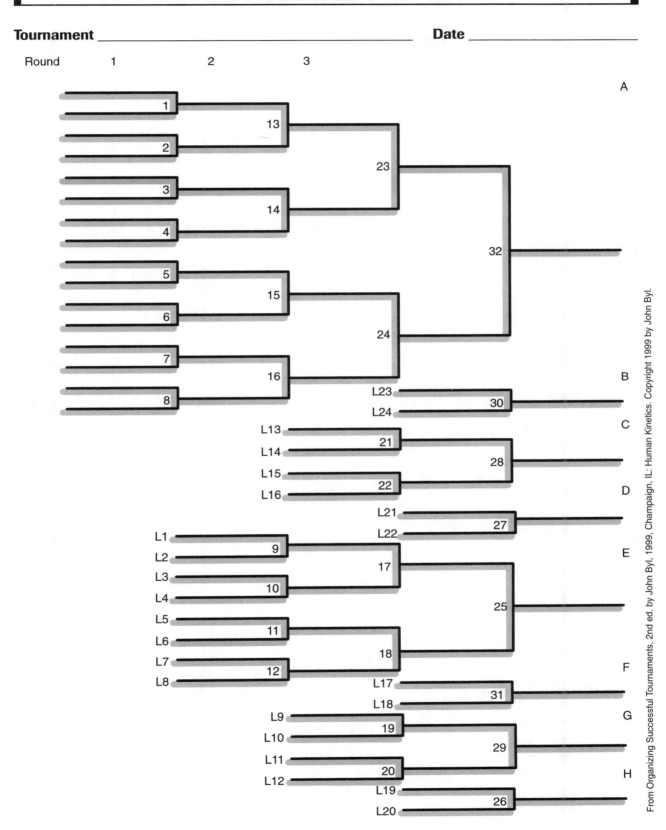

From Organizing Successful Tournaments, 2nd ed. by John Byl, 1999, Champaign, IL: Human Kinetics. Copyright 1999 by John Byl.

PLAYING SCHEDULES

Two Playing Areas

PA I	1	4	5	7
PA II	2	3	6	

Three Playing Areas

PA I	1	4	6	or	4	5
PA II	2	3	7		3	6
PA III		5				7

SEVEN ENTRIES

Two Playing Areas

PA I	1	3	6	7	9
PA II	2	4	5	8	

Three Playing Areas

PA I	1	6	9
PA II	2	5	8
PA III	3	4	7

EIGHT ENTRIES

Two Playing Areas

PA I	1	3	6	8	9	12
PA II	2	4	5	7	10	11

Three Playing Areas

PA I	1	4	6	8	12
PA II	2	5	7	9	11
PA III	3				10

Four Playing Areas

PA I	1	8	12
PA II	2	7	11
PA III	3	6	10
PA IV	4	5	9

NINE ENTRIES

Two Playing Areas

PA I	1	3	5	7	9	12	14
PA II	2	4	6	8	10	11	13

PLAYING SCHEDULES

Three Playing Areas

PA I	1	4	7	10	13
PA II	2	5	8	11	14
PA III	3	6	9	12	

Four Playing Areas

PA I	1	5	9	14
PA II	2	6	10	13
PA III	3	7	11	
PA IV	4	8	12	

Two Playing Areas

PA I	1	3	5	7	9	12	14	15
PA II	2	4	6	8	10	11	13	

Three Playing Areas

PA I	1	4	7	12	15
PA II	2	5	8	11	14
PA III	3	6	9	10	13

Four Playing Areas

PA I	1	5	9	15
PA II	2	6	10	14
PA III	3	7	11	13
PA IV	4	8	12	

Five Playing Areas

PA I	1	5	9	15	or	1	5	9	15
PA II	2	6	10	14		2	6	10	14
PA III	3	7	11			3	7		13
PA IV	4	8	12			4	8		12
PA V			13						11

Two Playing Areas

PA I	1	2	4	6	8	10	12	14	17
PA II		3	5	7	9	11	13	15	16

Three Playing Areas

PA I	1	4	7	10	15	17
PA II	2	5	8	11	14	16
PA III	3	6	9	12	13	

(continued)

Four Playing Areas

PA I	1	5	9	16	17
PA II	2	6	10	15	14
PA III	3	7	11		13
PA IV	4	8	12		

Five Playing Areas

PA I	1	6	9	17
PA II	2	7	10	16
PA III	3	8	11	15
PA IV	4		12	14
PA V	5			13

12 ENTRIES

Two Playing Areas

PA I	1	3	5	8	9	11	13	16	20	18
PA II	2	4	6	7	10	12	14	15	19	17

Three Playing Areas

PA I	1	4	8	10	13	16	18
PA II	2	5	7	11	14	20	17
PA III	3	6	9	12	15	19	

Four Playing Areas

PA I	1	5	9	13	17
PA II	2	6	10	14	18
PA III	3	7	11	15	19
PA IV	4	8	12	16	20

Five Playing Areas

PA I	1	6	10	14	18	or	1	5	9	13	18
PA II	2	7	11	15	17		2	6	10	14	17
PA III	3	8	12	16			3	7	11	15	16
PA IV	4	9	13	19			4	8	12		19
PA V	5			20							20

Six Playing Areas

PA I	1	8	11	15
PA II	2	7	12	16
PA III	3	9	13	17
PA IV	4	10	14	18
PA V	5			19
PA VI	6			20

PLAYING SCHEDULES

13 ENTRIES

Two Playing Areas

PA I	1	3	5	7	9	11	13	15	17	19	22
PA II	2	4	6	8	10	12	14	16	18	20	21

Three Playing Areas

PA I	1	4	7	10	13	16	19	22
PA II	2	5	8	11	14	17	20	
PA III	3	6	9	12	15	18	21	

Four Playing Areas

PA I	1	5	9	13	17	22	or	17	22
PA II	2	6	10	14	18	21		18	21
PA III	3	7	11	15	19				20
PA IV	4	8	12	16	20				19

Five Playing Areas

PA I	1	6	11	16	22	or	11	15	22
PA II	2	7	12	17	21		12	16	21
PA III	3	8	13	18			13	17	20
PA IV	4	9	14	19			14	18	19
PA V	5	10	15	20					

Six Playing Areas

PA I	1	7	12	22
PA II	2	8	13	21
PA III	3	9	14	20
PA IV	4	10	15	19
PA V	5	11	16	18
PA VI	6			17

14 ENTRIES

Two Playing Areas

PA I	1	2	4	6	8	10	12	14	16	18	20	22	25
PA II		3	5	7	9	11	13	15	17	19	21	23	24

Three Playing Areas

PA I	1	4	7	10	13	16	19	22	25
PA II	2	5	8	11	14	15	20	23	
PA III	3	6	9	12	17	18	21	24	

Four Playing Areas

PA I	1	5	9	13	17	21	25
PA II	2	6	10	14	18	22	
PA III	3	7	11	15	19	23	
PA IV	4	8	12	16	20	24	

(continued)

PLAYING SCHEDULES

Five Playing Areas

PA I	1	6	11	16	25
PA II	2	7	12	15	24
PA III	3	8	13	18	23
PA IV	4	9	14	19	22
PA V	5	10	17	20	21

Six Playing Areas

PA I	1	7	13	15	25
PA II	2	8	14	21	20
PA III	3	9	19	22	
PA IV	4	10	16	23	
PA V	5	11	17	24	
PA VI	6	12	18		

Seven Playing Areas

PA I	1	8	14	25
PA II	2	9	15	24
PA III	3	10	16	23
PA IV	4	11	17	22
PA V	5	12	18	21
PA VI	6	13	19	20
PA VII	7			

15 ENTRIES

Three Playing Areas

PA I	1	4	7	10	13	16	19	22	25	28
PA II	2	5	8	11	14	17	20	23	26	
PA III	3	6	9	12	15	18	21	24	27	

Four Playing Areas

PA I	1	5	9	13	17	21	28
PA II	2	6	10	14	18	22	27
PA III	3	7	11	15	19	23	26
PA IV	4	8	12	16	20	24	25

Five Playing Areas

PA I	1	6	11	16	21	28
PA II	2	7	12	17	22	27
PA III	3	8	13	18	23	26
PA IV	4	9	14	19	24	
PA V	5	10	15	20	25	

PLAYING SCHEDULES

Six Playing Areas

PA I	1	7	13	17	28	or	21	28
PA II	2	8	14	18	23		22	27
PA III	3	9	15	19	24		23	26
PA IV	4	10	16	20	25		24	25
PA V	5	11		21	26			
PA VI	6	12			27			

Seven Playing Areas

PA I	1	8	15	28
PA II	2	9	16	27
PA III	3	10	17	26
PA IV	4	11	18	25
PA V	5	12	19	24
PA VI	6	13	20	23
PA VII	7	14	21	22

16 ENTRIES

Three Playing Areas

PA I	1	4	7	10	13	16	19	22	27	30
PA II	2	5	8	11	14	17	20	23	26	29
PA III	3	6	9	12	15	18	21	24	25	28

Four Playing Areas

PA I	1	5	9	13	17	21	28	32
PA II	2	6	10	14	18	22	27	31
PA III	3	7	11	15	19	23	26	30
PA IV	4	8	12	16	20	24	25	29

Five Playing Areas

PA I	1	6	11	16	21	30	32
PA II	2	7	12	17	22	29	31
PA III	3	8	13	18	23	28	
PA IV	4	9	14	19	24	27	
PA V	5	10	15	20	25	26	

Six Playing Areas

PA I	1	7	13	19	30	32
PA II	2	8	14	20	29	31
PA III	3	9	15	21	28	
PA IV	4	10	16	22	27	
PA V	5	11	17	23	26	
PA VI	6	12	18	24	25	

(continued)

Seven Playing Areas

PA I	1	8	15	22	32
PA II	2	9	16	23	31
PA III	3	10	17	24	30
PA IV	4	11	18	25	29
PA V	5	12	19	26	
PA VI	6	13	20	27	
PA VII	7	14	21	28	

Eight Playing Areas

PA I	1	9	17	32
PA II	2	10	18	31
PA III	3	11	19	30
PA IV	4	12	20	29
PA V	5	13	21	28
PA VI	6	14	22	27
PA VII	7	15	23	26
PA VIII	8	16	24	25

CHAPTER 4

Double-Elimination Tournament

Advantages	Disadvantages
• Each entrant is guaranteed two games.	• Some players play many games; others play few.
• An entrant who loses once can still win the championship.	• It takes many rounds to complete.
• Seeding is not crucial.	• It does not maximize the use of multiple playing areas.
• It requires few playing areas.	
• Is a better measure of ability than single elimination.	

Best use: Situations in which time and playing areas are limited and final standings are important.

■ The top level of the double-elimination tournament is much the same as that of a single-elimination tournament, with only the final game being slightly different. Seeding is the same as for single elimination; we provide seeding charts for tournaments with 16 or fewer entries. Place the name of each player who wins on the draw sheet to the right of that player's previously recorded game. However, the first time an entry loses a game, the entry simply moves down to the appropriate position on the losers' bracket. Those who lose in the losers' bracket are eliminated (see figure 4.1). The ultimate winner of the losers' bracket has lost one game and can be eliminated only after losing twice. Therefore, this winner moves up to play the winner of the winners' bracket. If the winner of the losers' bracket wins this game, they must play one more game because the winner of the winners' bracket has lost only one game. This type of tournament requires many rounds, because for every round played on the winners' bracket, two must be played in the losers' bracket.

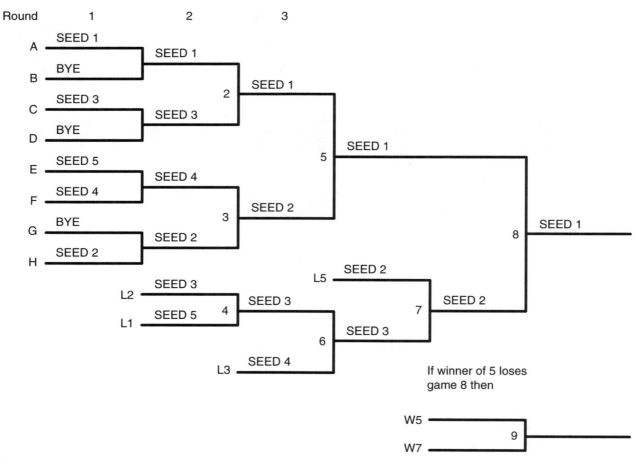

Figure 4.1 Double elimination—five entries.

To prevent players from playing each other twice in close succession, losers of a bracket cross over to the next major bracket. We have built this into the schedules, illustrated in figures 4.2, 4.3, and 4.4. However, there are three times when playing the same entry twice cannot be avoided. With correct seeding, the first- and second-seeded players will play each other twice; in fact, if these two entries split their games, they will play each other three times. The second situation in which two entries would play each other twice is when there are only

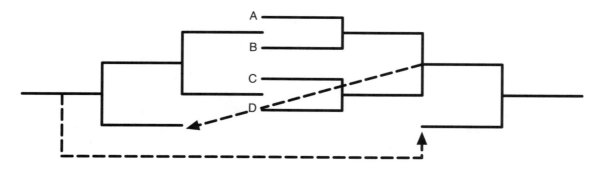

Figure 4.2 Double elimination—four or fewer entries.

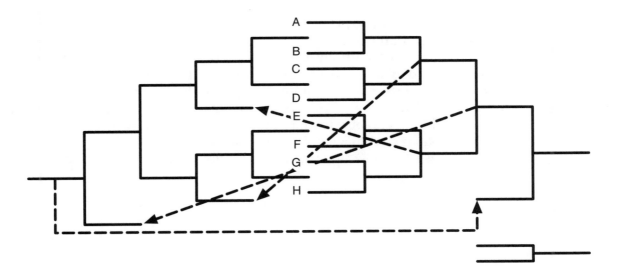

Figure 4.3 Double elimination—five to eight entries.

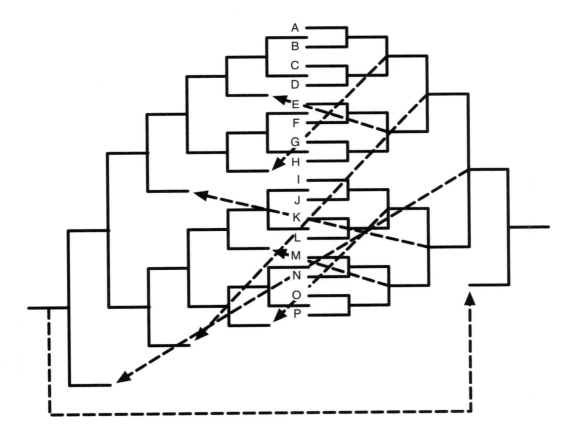

Figure 4.4 Double elimination—nine to sixteen entries.

three entries. Also, it is possible that lower seeded players who defeat higher seeded players in an early round will play their opponents twice.

The procedure for large, double-elimination tournaments is the same as for small ones. To conserve space, we have not prepared separate draw sheets for large numbers of entries. However, you can organize a tournament of this size easily in little additional time.

If you have more than 16 entries, for example 32 entries, it would be best to seed them into four double elimination draw sheets of eight entries each. The winners of those draws would be placed in a predetermined manner on a final draw sheet of four entries. If you had 64 entries you might select four draw sheets of 16 or eight draw sheets of eight, with winners going to a final draw sheet of either four or eight respectively. For other options on dealing with a large number of entries, see chapter 7.

If you wish to know how many games your tournament will require, the formula is as follows:

(Number of entries − 1) × 2 = number of games

Double-elimination tournament with three entries

Tournament _____ **Date** _____

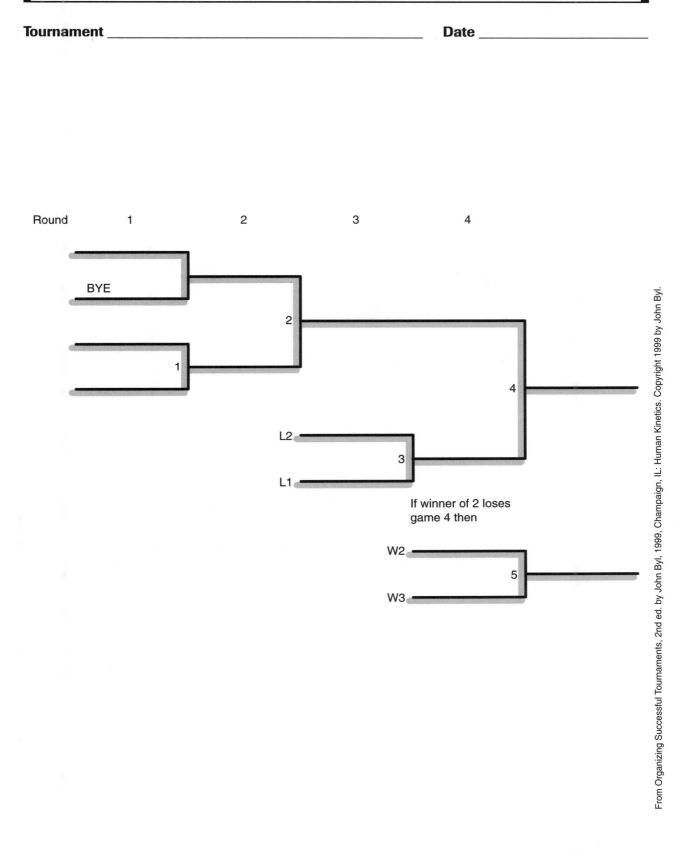

Round   1   2   3   4

BYE

2

1

L2

L1

3

4

If winner of 2 loses
game 4 then

W2

W3

5

From Organizing Successful Tournaments, 2nd ed. by John Byl, 1999, Champaign, IL: Human Kinetics. Copyright 1999 by John Byl.

Double-elimination tournament with four entries

Tournament _____ **Date** _____

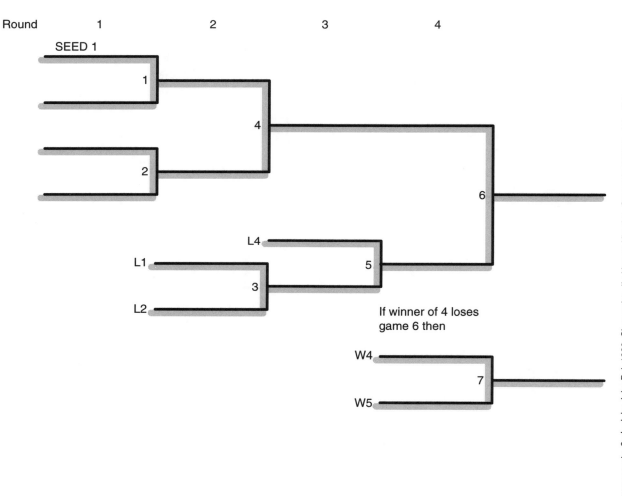

Round   1   2   3   4

SEED 1

1

2

4

L4

L1

3

L2

5

6

If winner of 4 loses
game 6 then

W4

W5

7

From Organizing Successful Tournaments, 2nd ed. by John Byl, 1999, Champaign, IL.: Human Kinetics. Copyright 1999 by John Byl.

Tournament _____ **Date** _____

Round   1   2   3   4   5   6

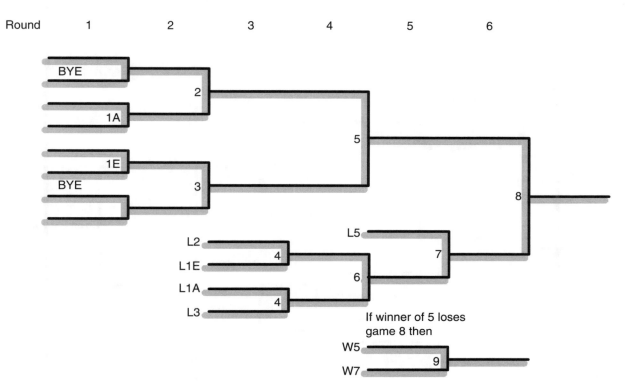

If winner of 5 loses game 8 then

From Organizing Successful Tournaments, 2nd ed. by John Byl, 1999, Champaign, IL: Human Kinetics. Copyright 1999 by John Byl.

Double-elimination tournament with six entries

Tournament _____ **Date** _____

Round   1   2   3   4   5   6

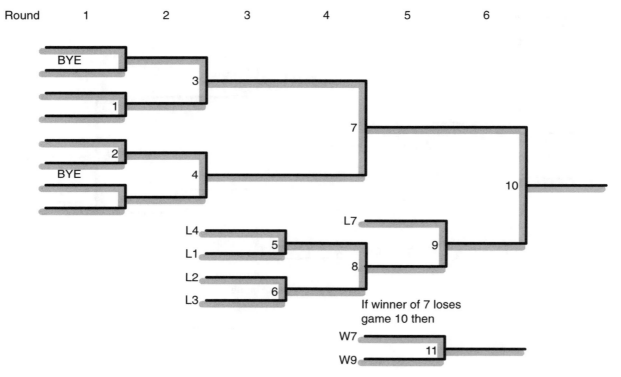

If winner of 7 loses game 10 then

From Organizing Successful Tournaments, 2nd ed. by John Byl, 1999, Champaign, IL: Human Kinetics. Copyright 1999 by John Byl.

Double-elimination tournament with seven entries

Tournament _____ **Date** _____

Round   1   2   3   4   5   6

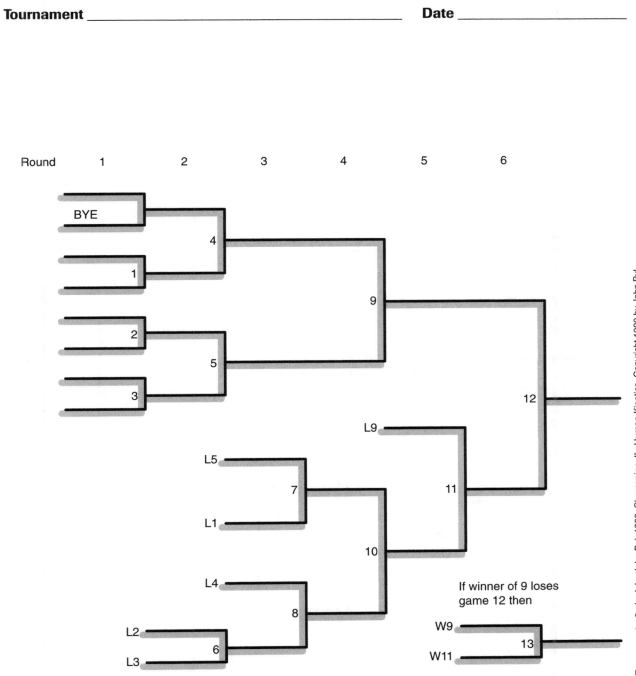

If winner of 9 loses
game 12 then

From Organizing Successful Tournaments, 2nd ed. by John Byl, 1999, Champaign, IL: Human Kinetics. Copyright 1999 by John Byl.

Double-elimination tournament with eight entries

Tournament _____   **Date** _____

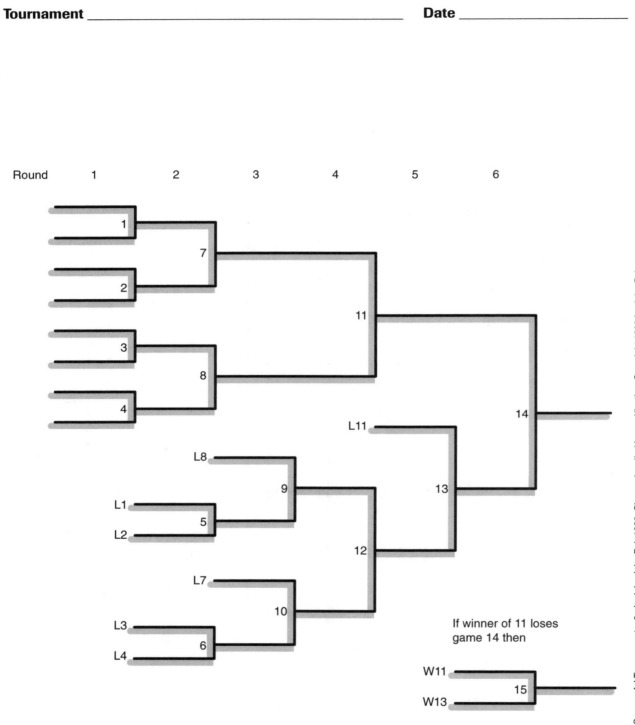

Round   1   2   3   4   5   6

If winner of 11 loses
game 14 then

From Organizing Successful Tournaments, 2nd ed. by John Byl, 1999, Champaign, IL: Human Kinetics. Copyright 1999 by John Byl.

Double-elimination tournament with nine entries

Tournament _____ **Date** _____

Round   1   2   3   4   5   6   7   8

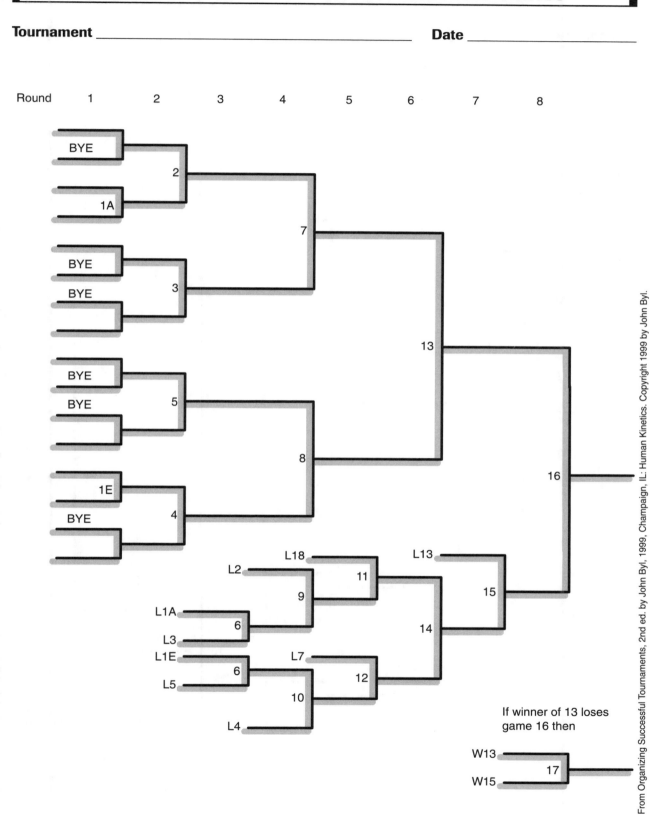

If winner of 13 loses
game 16 then

W13
W15
17

From Organizing Successful Tournaments, 2nd ed. by John Byl, 1999, Champaign, IL: Human Kinetics. Copyright 1999 by John Byl.

Double-elimination tournament with 10 entries

Tournament _____ **Date** _____

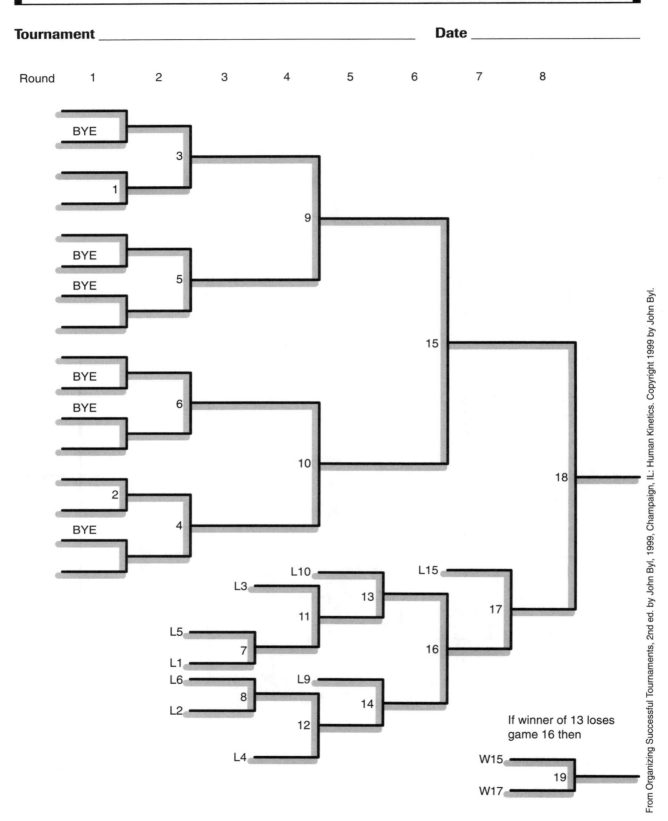

Round   1   2   3   4   5   6   7   8

BYE
3
1

9

BYE
5
BYE

15

BYE
6
BYE

10

2
4
BYE

18

L10
L3
13
11

L15

17

L5
7
L1

16

L6
8
L2

L9
14

12

L4

If winner of 13 loses game 16 then

W15
19
W17

From Organizing Successful Tournaments, 2nd ed. by John Byl, 1999, Champaign, IL: Human Kinetics. Copyright 1999 by John Byl.

Double-elimination tournament with 11 entries

Tournament _____ Date _____

Round 1 2 3 4 5 6 7 8

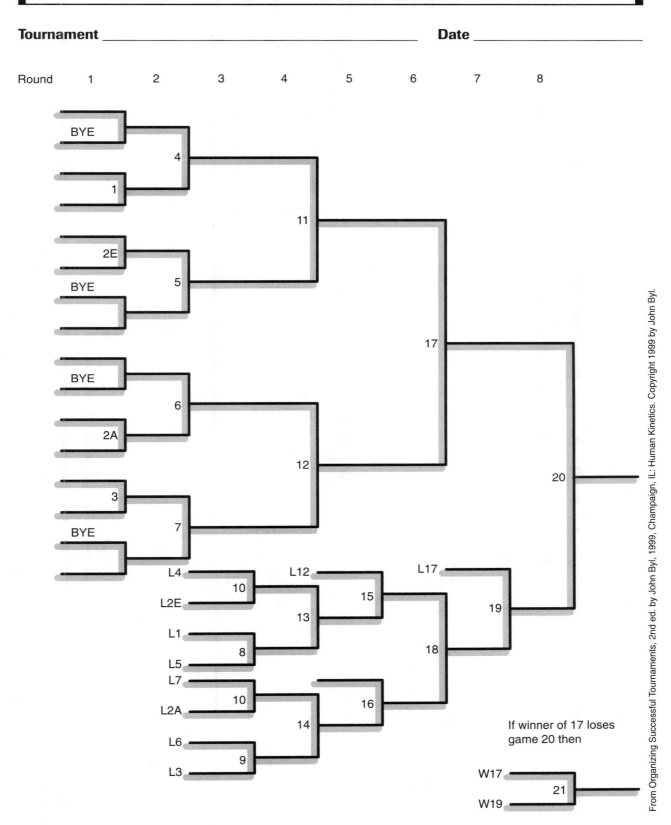

If winner of 17 loses game 20 then

From Organizing Successful Tournaments, 2nd ed. by John Byl, 1999, Champaign, IL: Human Kinetics. Copyright 1999 by John Byl.

Double-elimination tournament with 12 entries

Tournament _____ **Date** _____

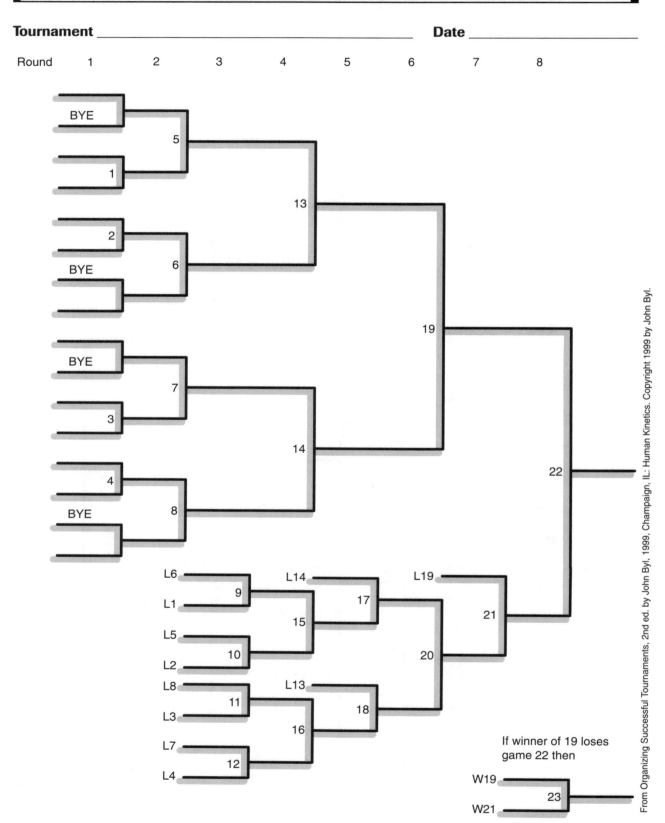

Round   1   2   3   4   5   6   7   8

If winner of 19 loses
game 22 then

From Organizing Successful Tournaments, 2nd ed. by John Byl, 1999, Champaign, IL: Human Kinetics. Copyright 1999 by John Byl.

Double-elimination tournament with 13 entries

Tournament _____ Date _____

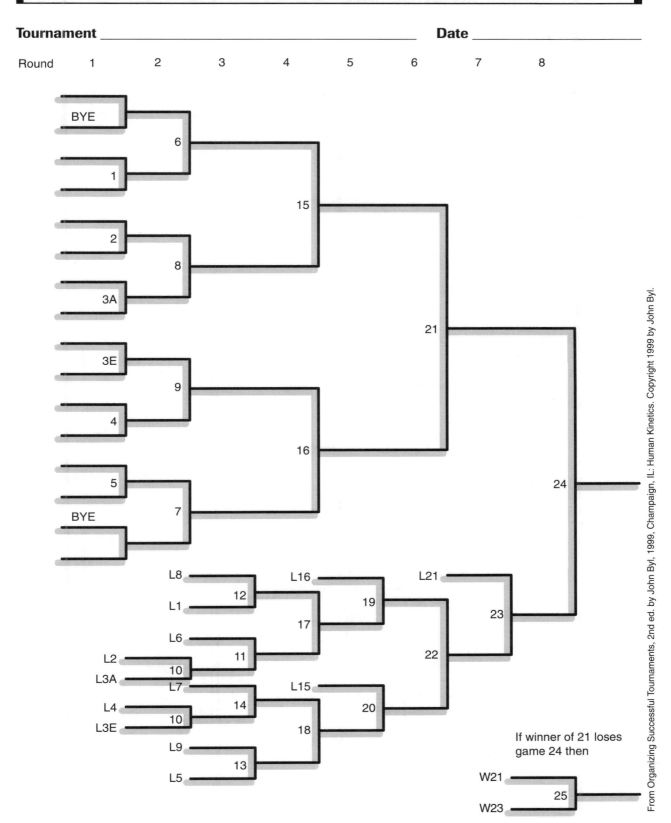

Round   1   2   3   4   5   6   7   8

If winner of 21 loses
game 24 then

From Organizing Successful Tournaments, 2nd ed. by John Byl, 1999, Champaign, IL: Human Kinetics. Copyright 1999 by John Byl.

Double-elimination tournament with 14 entries

Tournament _____ Date _____

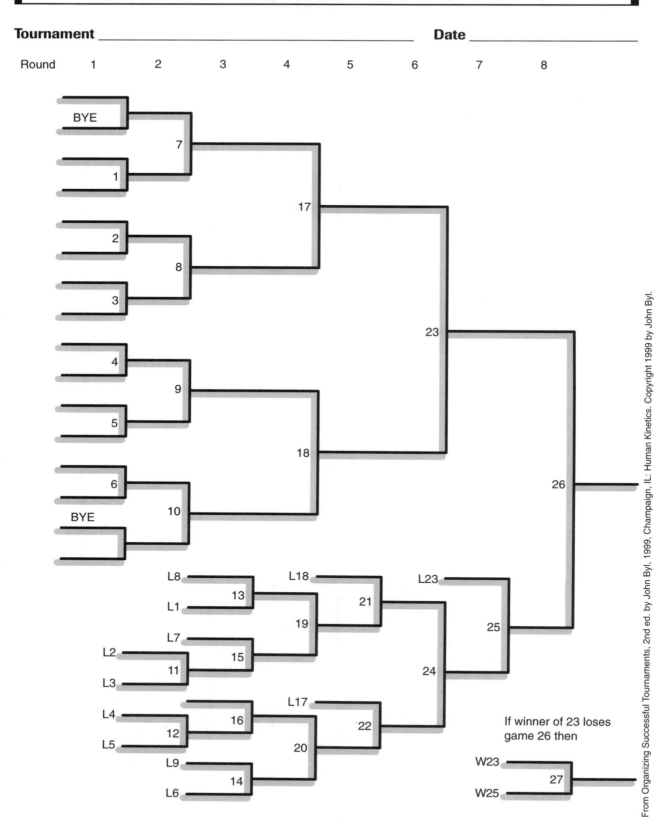

Round   1   2   3   4   5   6   7   8

If winner of 23 loses
game 26 then

From Organizing Successful Tournaments, 2nd ed. by John Byl, 1999, Champaign, IL: Human Kinetics. Copyright 1999 by John Byl.

Double-elimination tournament with 15 entries

Tournament _____ **Date** _____

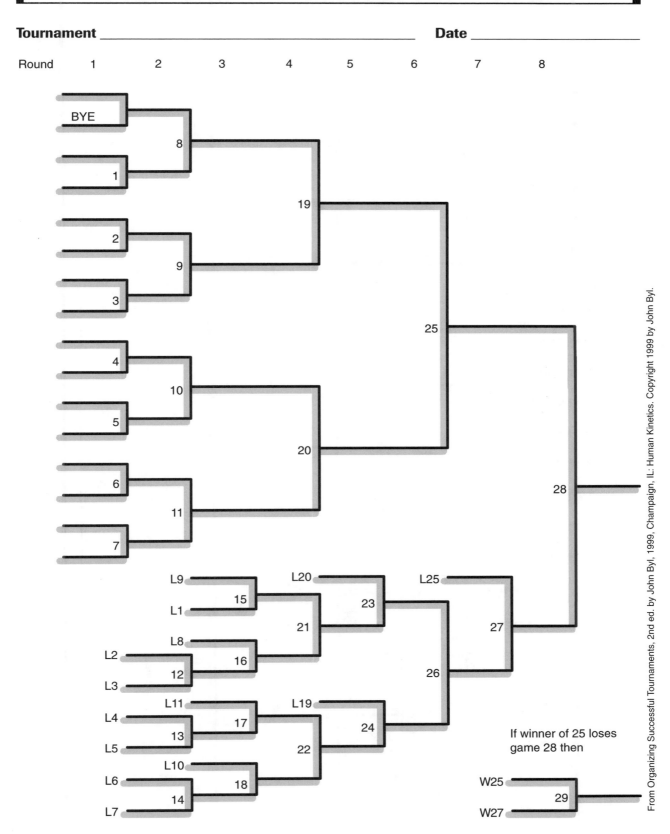

Round   1   2   3   4   5   6   7   8

BYE

If winner of 25 loses
game 28 then

From Organizing Successful Tournaments, 2nd ed. by John Byl, 1999, Champaign, IL: Human Kinetics. Copyright 1999 by John Byl.

Double-elimination tournament with 16 entries

Tournament _____ **Date** _____

Round   1   2   3   4   5   6   7   8

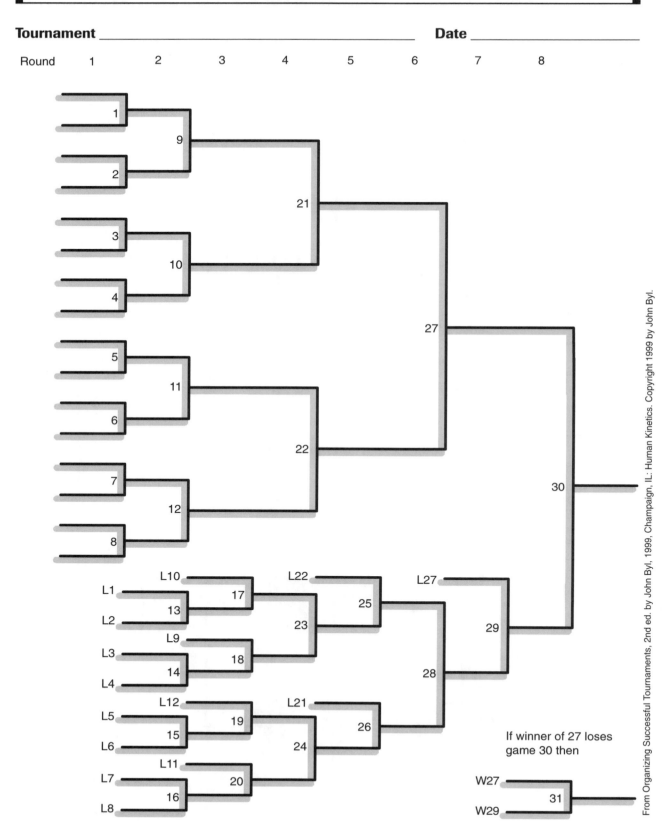

If winner of 27 loses game 30 then

From Organizing Successful Tournaments, 2nd ed. by John Byl, 1999, Champaign, IL.: Human Kinetics. Copyright 1999 by John Byl.

PLAYING SCHEDULES

THREE ENTRIES

One Playing Area

PA I	1	2	3	4	(5)

FOUR ENTRIES

Two Playing Areas

PA I	1	3	5	6	(7)
PA II	2	4			

FIVE ENTRIES

Two Playing Areas

PA I	1	3	5	7	8	(9)
PA II	2	4	6			

SIX ENTRIES

Two Playing Areas

PA I	1	4	5	7	9	10	(11)
PA II	2	3	6	8			

SEVEN ENTRIES

Two Playing Areas

PA I	1	4	5	7	9	11	12	(13)
PA II	2	3	6	8	10			

Three Playing Areas

PA I	1	4	7	9	11	12	(13)	
PA II	2	5	8	10				
PA III	3	6						

EIGHT ENTRIES

Two Playing Areas

PA I	1	3	5	7	9	11	13	14	(15)
PA II	2	4	6	8	10	12			

Three Playing Areas

PA I	1	4	7	10	12	13	14	(15)
PA II	2	5	8	11				
PA III	3		6	9				

(continued)

Four Playing Areas

PA I	1	5	11	12	13	14	(15)
PA II	2	6	10				
PA III	3	7	9				
PA IV	4	8					

NINE ENTRIES

Two Playing Areas

PA I	1	3	5	7	9	11	13	15	16	(17)
PA II	2	4	6	8	10	12	14			

Three Playing Areas

PA I	1	4	7	9	11	13	15	16	(17)
PA II	2	5	8	10	12	14			
PA III	3	6							

Four Playing Areas

PA I	1	5	8	11	13	15	16	(17)
PA II	2	6	9	12	14			
PA III	3	7	10					
PA IV	4							

10 ENTRIES

Two Playing Areas

PA I	1	3	5	7	9	11	13	15	17	18	(19)
PA II	2	4	6	8	10	12	14	16			

Three Playing Areas

PA I	1	4	7	10	13	15	17	18	(19)
PA II	2	5	8	11	14	16			
PA III	3	6	9	12					

Four Playing Areas

PA I	1	5	9	13	15	17	18	(19)
PA II	2	6	10	14	16			
PA III	3	7	11					
PA IV	4	8	12					

11 ENTRIES

Two Playing Areas

PA I	1	3	5	7	9	11	13	15	17	19	20	(21)
PA II	2	4	6	8	10	12	14	16	18			

Three Playing Areas

PA I	1	4	7	10	13	15	18	19	20	(21)
PA II	2	5	8	11	14	16				
PA III	3	6	9	12		17				

Four Playing Areas

PA I	1	5	9	13	15	18	19	(21)
PA II	2	6	10	14	16			
PA III	3	7	11		17			
PA IV	4	8	12					

12 ENTRIES

Two Playing Areas

PA I	1	3	5	7	9	11	13	15	17	19	21	22	(23)
PA II	2	4	6	8	10	12	14	16	18	20			

Three Playing Areas

PA I	1	4	7	10	13	16	18	20	21	22	(23)
PA II	2	5	8	11	14	17	19				
PA III	3	6	9	12	15						

Four Playing Areas

PA I	1	5	9	13	17	19	21	22	(23)
PA II	2	6	10	14	18	20			
PA III	3	7	11	15					
PA IV	4	8	12	16					

13 ENTRIES

Two Playing Areas

PA I	1	3	5	7	9	11	13	15	17	19	21	23	24	(25)
PA II	2	4	6	8	10	12	14	16	18	20	22			

Three Playing Areas

PA I	1	4	7	10	13	16	19	22	23	24	(25)
PA II	2	5	8	11	14	17	20				
PA III	3	6	9	12	15	18	21				

Four Playing Areas

PA I	1	5	9	13	17	19	22	23	24	(25)
PA II	2	6	10	14	18	20				
PA III	3	7	11	15		21				
PA IV	4	8	12	16						

(continued)

PLAYING SCHEDULES

Five Playing Areas

PA I	1	6	11	16	19	22	23	24	(25)
PA II	2	7	12	17	20				
PA III	3	8	13	18	21				
PA IV	4	9	14						
PA V	5	10	15						

14 ENTRIES

Two Playing Areas

PA I	1	3	5	7	9	11	13	15	17	19	21	23	25	26	(27)
PA II	2	4	6	8	10	12	14	16	18	20	22	24			

Three Playing Areas

PA I	1	4	7	10	13	16	19	21	23	25	26	(27)
PA II	2	5	8	11	14	17	20	22	24			
PA III	3	6	9	12	15	18						

Four Playing Areas

PA I	1	5	9	13	17	21	23	25	26	(27)
PA II	2	6	10	14	18	22	24			
PA III	3	7	11	15	19					
PA IV	4	8	12	16	20					

Five Playing Areas

PA I	1	6	10	15	19	21	23	25	26	(27)
PA II	2	7	11	16	20	22	24			
PA III	3	8	12	17						
PA IV	4	9	13	18						
PA V	5		14							

Six Playing Areas

PA I	1	7	13	19	21	23	25	26	(27)
PA II	2	8	14	20	22	24			
PA III	3	9	15						
PA IV	4	10	16						
PA V	5	11	17						
PA VI	6	12	18						

15 ENTRIES

Two Playing Areas

PA I	1	3	5	7	9	11	13	15	17	19	21	23	25	27	28	(29)
PA II	2	4	6	8	10	12	14	16	18	20	22	24	26			

PLAYING SCHEDULES

Three Playing Areas

PA I	1	4	7	10	13	16	19	22	24	26	27	28	(29)
PA II	2	5	8	11	14	17	20	23	25				
PA III	3	6	9	12	15	18	21						

Four Playing Areas

PA I	1	5	9	13	17	21	23	25	27	28	(29)
PA II	2	6	10	14	18	22	24	26			
PA III	3	7	11	15	19						
PA IV	4	8	12	16	20						

Five Playing Areas

PA I	1	6	10	15	20	23	25	27	28	(29)
PA II	2	7	11	16	21	24	26			
PA III	3	8	12	17	22					
PA IV	4	9	13	18						
PA V	5		14	19						

Six Playing Areas

PA I	1	7	11	16	21	23	25	27	28	(29)
PA II	2	8	12	17	22	24	26			
PA III	3	9	13	18						
PA IV	4	10	14	19						
PA V	5		15	20						
PA VI	6									

Seven Playing Areas

PA I	1	8	15	21	23	25	27	28	(29)
PA II	2	9	16	22	24	26			
PA III	3	10	17						
PA IV	5	12	19						
PA V	6	13	20						
PA VI	7	14							

16 ENTRIES

Two Playing Areas

PA I	1	4	7	10	13	16	19	22	25	28	29	30	(31)
PA II	2	5	8	11	14	17	20	23	26				
PA III	3	6	9	12	15	18	21	24	27				

Four Playing Areas

PA I	1	5	9	13	17	21	25	28	29	30	(31)
PA II	2	6	10	14	18	22	26				
PA III	3	7	11	15	19	23	27				
PA IV	4	8	12	16	20	24					

(continued)

PLAYING SCHEDULES

Five Playing Areas

PA I	1	6	11	16	20	24	26	28	29	30	(31)
PA II	2	7	12	17	21	25	27			
PA III	3	8	13	18	22					
PA IV	4	9	14	19	23					
PA V	5	10	15							

Six Playing Areas

PA I	1	7	13	17	21	25	27	29	30	(31)
PA II	2	8	14	18	22	26	28		
PA III	3	9	15	19	23				
PA IV	4	10	16	20	24				
PA V	5	11	12						
PA VI	6								

Seven Playing Areas

PA I	1	8	15	19	24	26	28	29	30	(31)
PA II	2	9	16	20	25	27			
PA III	3	10	17	21					
PA IV	4	11	18	22					
PA V	5	13	12	23					
PA VI	6	14							
PA VII	7								

Eight Playing Areas

PA I	1	9	17	23	25	28	29	30	(31)
PA II	2	10	18	24	26			
PA III	3	11	19	27				
PA IV	4	12	20					
PA V	5	13	21					
PA VI	6	14	22					
PA VII	7	15						
PA VIII	8	16						

CHAPTER 5

Round Robin Tournament

Round Robin

Advantages

- All players play each other, so true standings result.
- Seeding is unimportant.
- It uses multiple playing areas effectively.
- No one is eliminated.

Disadvantages

- It requires many games.
- Many games may be lopsided.

Best use: League play and whenever true standings are essential

---

Round Robin-Split

Advantages

- It requires fewer games than round robin.

Disadvantages

- Proper seeding is important.

Best use: League play and whenever true standings are essential, but time or space is limited.

■ Round robin play involves each entry playing all other entries. Round robin tournaments with many entries take a long time to complete. If you wish to use this tournament with a large number of entries, the best strategy is to divide the entries into two, three, or four pools. In this chapter we explain the round robin tournament, and the variations with pool play, and include necessary schedules and support materials.

Although much of the following discussion deals with a one- or two-day tournament, this type of tournament could also form the schedule for an entire season of play. Some schedules included in this chapter have identifying marks to assist in planning a league schedule. You will find one schedule for each number of entries marked as follows: Rounds are separated by lines, and a • (bullets refer to home games) identifies the home team. For home and away games, you simply repeat the schedule and make the • team the visiting team.

Seeding is unimportant to the final outcome of round robin; however, the tournament might be more interesting if the deciding games are at the end—so that in the final game seed 1 plays seed 2, 3 plays 4, 5 plays 6, and so on. To accommodate this, we have provided a seeding chart. Once you have decided to seed or not to seed, you can place the player names in the correct spots on the appropriate recording sheet. Figure 5.5 (pg. 96) present recording sheets for tournaments of up to 4 entries, 8 entries, and 16 entries, respectively.

We have prepared the playing schedules to make your work easier and more precise. To simplify things for the participants, provide them with a filled-in schedule as shown in figure 5.1. Beyond having the deciding games be the finals,

A. Canadore
B. Redeemer
C. Cambrian
D. Niagara

	Court I	Court II
10:00 am	Canadore-Cambrian	Redeemer-Niagara
11:15 am	Redeemer-Cambrian	Canadore-Niagara
12:30 pm	Canadore-Redeemer	Cambrian-Niagara

Figure 5.1 Ontario College Athletic Association Men's Volleyball Tournament, Redeemer College, January 28, 1998.

two other principles influenced the organization of the playing schedules. The first is to minimize the number of games any team plays in a row. Although it is unavoidable for teams to play several games in a row, we made every attempt to equalize that among all the teams. The second principle is to equalize the number of games each entry plays on each playing area. (If one playing area in the tournament is the most or least undesirable, it would hardly be fair for any entry to be advantaged or disadvantaged by playing a high percentage of its games on that court.)

You may need to build in a rest period, especially when playing with the maximum number of playing areas. You can facilitate this rest period as a rule stating that all entries may have a minimum of so many minutes rest between games. Or, you may wish to establish longer breaks at certain points in the tournament, perhaps following every fourth match.

Because all entries play each other, the final ranking is determined by the cumulative outcome of all games. Usually 2 points are awarded for a win, 1 point for a tie, and 0 points for a loss. Should there be a tie in the standings, you may turn for help to the appendix, which outlines various tiebreaking procedures for tournaments.

Should you decide to make your own schedule, take the following into account.

1. Use rotations to ensure that all entries play each other. The schedules presented in this chapter use the following rotations:

If there is an even number, A stays while the others rotate clockwise.

$$\begin{matrix} A & B \\ \nearrow & \downarrow \\ C & \leftarrow D \end{matrix} \qquad \begin{matrix} A & C \\ \nearrow & \downarrow \\ D & \leftarrow B \end{matrix} \qquad \begin{matrix} A & D \\ \nearrow & \downarrow \\ B & \leftarrow C \end{matrix}$$

If there is an odd number, X stays while the others rotate clockwise.

$$\begin{matrix} A & \rightarrow B \\ \nwarrow & \downarrow \\ X & C \end{matrix} \qquad \begin{matrix} C & \rightarrow A \\ \nwarrow & \downarrow \\ X & B \end{matrix} \qquad \begin{matrix} B & \rightarrow C \\ \nwarrow & \downarrow \\ X & A \end{matrix}$$

This rotation ensures that all entries play each other, but it leaves uneven schedules. For example, one team might play four games in a row, have three breaks, then play another four, while another playing unit might have two games, one break, two games, one break, two games, one break, and two games. The latter has a far superior schedule. To balance this as much as possible, we rearranged the schedules in this manual.

2. The playing areas of some tournaments may vary in quality. To balance this, the entries are further rearranged. If more than 16 entries will participate, the tournament would likely become excessively long. Sixteen entries requires 120 games. It is unlikely that you would wish to exceed this number and still use the round robin approach. Instead, you would be better off to split the group into two, three, or four pools and use one of the approaches suggested in the next few pages.

The calculation for determining the number of games is this:

[Entries × (Entries – 1)]/2 = Games

Round Robin-Double Split

The round robin-double split is simply a round robin tournament with the entries split into two pools or divisions. The principles and procedures are the same as for the round robin, but there are some differences that we should note.

There are two pools, and each needs it own recording sheet. The seeding is also different; at the end of pool play, the top players from one pool play the top players from the other pool to determine overall tournament ranking. As in single elimination, the top-ranked player goes in the first pool, the second in the second pool, the third in the first pool, and so on. If this were not done, major problems might develop. For example, if we had eight entries and placed the top four in pool 1 and the bottom four in pool 2, the third-and fourth-ranked entries would not make it to the finals. Instead, at best the fifth- and sixth-ranked entries would, and this is obviously undesirable. The seeding chart on page 89 will help you do seeding and placement. To use the equitable seeding format, simply switch 1 and 2. This will make 1 play 3 and 2 play 4 in the play-offs but will also give 1 an additional game—probably not desirable.

Various kinds of play-offs are possible. The ones listed on the following pages are single elimination in format and are the most commonly used. The play-off format in figure 5.2 involves the top two from each pool, plus a third-place match. This approach is useful not only for determining the top standings but also for providing a break for the top two teams, especially if only one playing area is available. The second play-off format, in figure 5.3, includes the top four from each pool playing in an eight-entry, single-elimination play-off with a third-place match. This approach works effectively when the number of entries is small and equality in numbers of games per entry is important. For example, if you had six entries, dividing them into two pools would assure all entries of two games. However, if you then went to a play-off that included a third-place match, with only the top two of each pool advancing, the top four entries of the tournament would play four games each while the bottom two would play only twice. This would take 10 games. If instead you used the eight-entry play-offs minus the third-place match and placed all the entries on the play-off draw sheet, giving a bye to the top-place finisher in each pool, only one game would be added to the entire schedule and the bottom two entries would receive one more game.

In pool play it is often advantageous, for scheduling and player interest, to play as many as possible of the intrapool games on the same playing areas. If many playing areas are available, assign each pool several playing areas, and evenly distribute entries.

To determine the number of games required, calculate the number of games per pool, using the round robin formula on page 87, then add the number of games required for the appropriate play-off format:

Pool 1 + pool 2 + play-offs = number of games

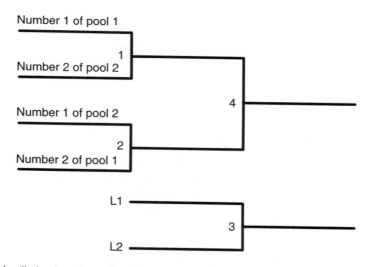

Figure 5.2 Single elimination play-offs with third-place match (round robin double-split).

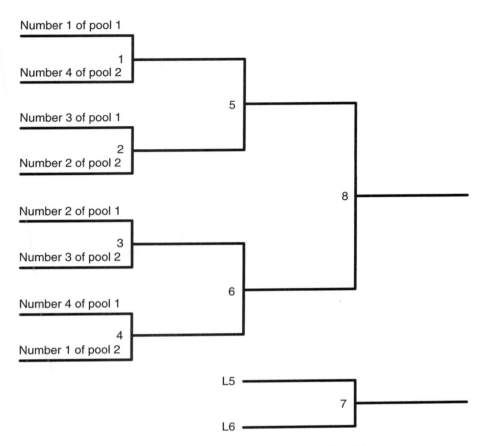

Number 1 of pool 1

Number 4 of pool 2

Number 3 of pool 1

Number 2 of pool 2

Number 2 of pool 1

Number 3 of pool 2

Number 4 of pool 1

Number 1 of pool 2

Figure 5.3   Single elimination play-offs with third-place match (round robin triple-split).

Round Robin-Triple Split

The round robin-triple split is a round robin tournament with the entries split into three pools or divisions. The principles and procedures for placing the entries into pools are basically the same as for the round robin-double split, but there are some differences. As with any round robin, you could use this format for a one- or two-day tournament or as the structure for league play involving three pools or divisions.

Each pool needs its own recording sheet. The seeding procedure places each of the top three seeds into a different pool, then follows that pattern for the lower seeds (see the seeding chart on page 91.

Various kinds of play-offs are possible, two of which we include in this chapter. One option is simply to take the top finisher of each pool and have them play each other in a three-game round robin. However, if you seeded incorrectly, the second-best player may have been in the same pool as the number one seed. That play-off would then prove unsatisfactory because there would be no opportunity for the second-best player to make it into the play-offs. The preferred play-off is one in which the top two entries from each pool advance. Though you could use a single-elimination play-off with six entries, which would shorten the number of games played, a round robin play-off for the remaining six entries is most desirable.

To determine the number of games required, calculate the number of games per pool using the round robin formula on page 87, then add the number of games required for the appropriate play-off format:

Pool 1 + pool 2 + pool 3 + play-offs = number of games

Round Robin-Quadruple Split

The round robin-quadruple split is a round robin tournament with the entries split into four pools or divisions. The principles and procedures for placing the entries into pools are basically the same as for the other round robin-split tournaments, but there are some differences.

The seeding process is the same as for the round robin-triple split, and the seeding charts are included on the following pages.

We have included one play-off format (see figure 5.4). It would be possible to have only the top finisher in each pool advance to the play-offs, but for reasons of fairness explained earlier, this would be undesirable. You do have the option of eliminating the third-place match if necessary. If there are only 12 entries in a tournament, you may also wish to extend the play-offs to include all players, but this would obviously make a longer tournament, and perhaps a round robin-double split would be a better choice.

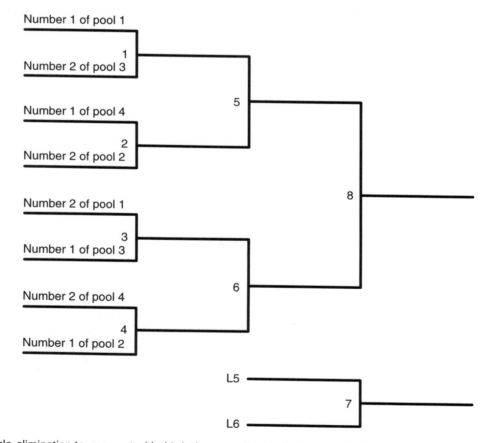

Figure 5.4 Single-elimination tournament with third-place match (round robin-quadruple split).

To determine the number of games required, calculate the number of games per pool, using the round robin formula on page 87, then add the number of games required for the appropriate play-off format:

Pool 1 + pool 2 + pool 3 + pool 4 + play-offs = number of games

Starting position	Number of entries													
	3	**4**	**5**	**6**	**7**	**8**	**9**	**10**	**11**	**12**	**13**	**14**	**15**	**16**
A	1	3	1	5	3	7	5	9	7	11	9	13	11	15
B	3	4	3	3	5	5	7	7	9	9	11	11	13	13
C	2	1	5	1	1	3	3	5	5	7	7	9	9	11
D		2	4	6	6	8	8	10	10	12	13	14	14	16
E			2	2	7	1	1	3	3	5	5	7	7	9
F				4	4	6	6	8	8	10	12	12	12	14
G				2	2	9	1	1	3	3	5	5	7
H						4	4	6	6	8	10	10	10	12
I							2	2	11	1	1	3	3	5
J								4	4	6	8	8	8	10
K									2	2	2	1	1	3
L										4	6	6	6	8
M											4	2	15	1
N												4	4	6
O													2	2
P														4

Seeding For Round Robin-Double Split Tournaments

Pool	Starting position	Number of entries										
		6	7	8	9	10	11	12	13	14	15	16
1	A	1	1	5	5	1	1	9	9	5	5	13
	B	5	5	7	7	5	5	5	5	9	9	9
	C	3	3	1	1	9	9	1	1	1	1	5
	D			3	3	7	7	11	11	11	11	15
	E					3	3	3	3	13	13	1
	F							7	7	7	7	11
	G									3	3	3
	H											7
2	A	2	6	6	2	2	10	10	6	6	14	14
	B	6	7	8	6	6	6	6	10	10	10	10
	C	4	2	2	9	10	2	2	2	2	6	6
	D		4	4	8	8	11	12	12	12	15	16
	E				4	4	4	4	13	14	2	2
	F						8	8	8	8	12	12
	G								4	4	4	4
	H										8	8

Seeding For Round Robin-Triple Split Tournaments

Pool	Starting position	Number of entries							
		9	10	11	12	13	14	15	16
1	A	1	1	1	7	7	7	1	1
	B	7	7	7	10	10	10	7	7
	C	4	4	4	1	1	1	13	13
	D				4	4	4	10	10
	E							4	4
	F								
2	A	2	2	8	8	8	2	2	2
	B	8	8	10	11	11	8	8	8
	C	5	5	2	2	2	13	14	14
	D			5	5	5	11	11	11
	E						5	5	5
	F								
3	A	3	9	9	9	3	3	3	15
	B	9	10	11	12	9	9	9	9
	C	6	3	3	3	13	14	15	3
	D		6	6	6	12	12	12	16
	E					6	6	6	6
	F								12

Equitable Seeding for Round Robin– Quadruple Split Tournaments

Pool	Starting position	Number of entries				
		12	**13**	**14**	**15**	**16**
1	**A**	1	1	1	1	9
	B	9	9	9	9	13
	C	5	5	5	5	1
	D					5
2	**A**	2	2	2	10	10
	B	10	10	10	13	14
	C	6	6	6	2	2
	D				6	6
3	**A**	3	3	11	11	11
	B	11	11	13	14	15
	C	7	7	3	3	3
	D			7	7	7
4	**A**	4	12	12	12	12
	B	12	13	14	15	16
	C	8	4	4	4	4
	D		8	8	8	8

Pool	Starting position	Number of entries				
		12	**13**	**14**	**15**	**16**
1	**A**	1	1	1	1	1
	B	12	12	12	12	16
	C	6	6	6	6	12
	D					6
2	**A**	2	2	2	11	11
	B	11	11	11	15	15
	C	5	5	5	2	2
	D				5	5
3	**A**	3	3	9	9	9
	B	9	9	14	14	14
	C	8	8	3	3	3
	D			8	8	8
4	**A**	4	10	10	10	10
	B	10	13	13	13	13
	C	7	4	4	4	4
	D		7	7	7	7

Advantage Seeding for Round Robin– Quadruple Split Tournaments

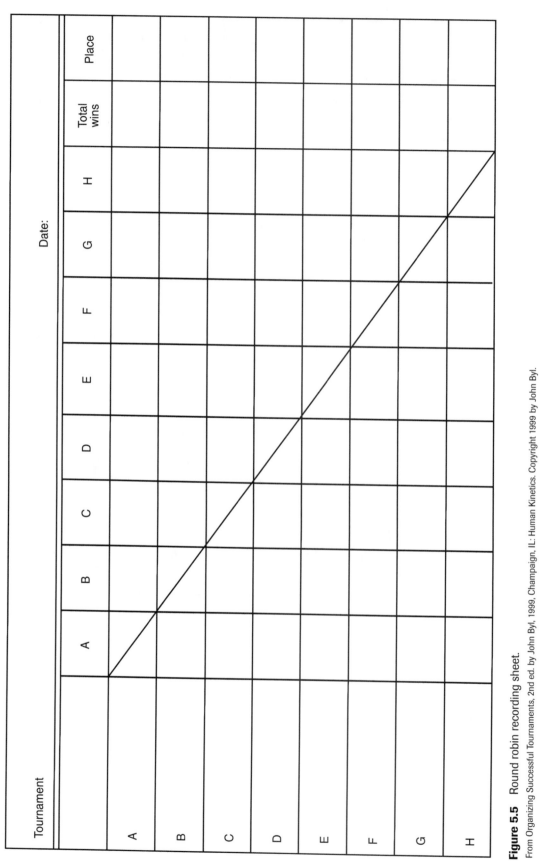

Figure 5.5 Round robin recording sheet.

From Organizing Successful Tournaments, 2nd ed. by John Byl, 1999, Champaign, IL: Human Kinetics. Copyright 1999 by John Byl.

PLAYING SCHEDULES
FOR ROUND ROBIN TOURNAMENTS

THREE ENTRIES

One Playing Area

PA I
1 •A-B
--
2 •B-C
--
3 A-C•

FOUR ENTRIES

One Playing Area

PA I
1 •A-C
2 •B-D
--
3 A-D•
4 B-C•
--
5 •A-B
6 •C-D

Two Playing Areas

PA I	PA II
1 A-C	2 B-D
3 B-C	4 A-D
5 A-B	6 C-D

FIVE ENTRIES

One Playing Area

PA I
1 •A-D
2 •B-C
--
3 •D-E
4 A-C•
--
5 B-E•
6 C-D•
--
7 •A-B
8 •C-E
--
9 •B-D
10 A-E•

Two Playing Areas

PA I	PA II
1 A-D	2 B-C
3 A-C	4 D-E
5 B-E	6 C-D
7 C-E	8 A-B
9 B-D	10 A-E

SIX ENTRIES

One Playing Area

PA I
1 •A-B
2 C-D•
3 •E-F
--
4 A-C•
5 •B-E
6 D-F•
--
7 •A-E
8 •C-F
9 B-D•
--
10 A-F•
11 D-E•
12 •B-C
--
13 •A-D
14 •B-F
15 •C-E

Two Playing Areas

PA I	PA II
1 A-B	
2 C-D	3 E-F
4 D-F	5 A-E
6 B-E	7 A-C
8 C-F	9 B-D
10 A-F	11 D-E
12 A-D	13 B-C
14 C-E	15 B-F

Three Playing Areas

PA I	PA II	PA III
1 A-B	2 E-F	3 C-D
4 D-F	5 A-C	6 B-E
7 A-E	8 B-D	9 C-F
10 B-C	11 D-E	12 A-F
13 C-E	14 B-F	15 A-D

Note: • = indicates home team for league play
         – = indicates new round for league play

(continued)

PLAYING SCHEDULES

FOR ROUND ROBIN TOURNAMENTS

SEVEN ENTRIES

One Playing Area

PA I
1 B-C•
2 •D-G
3 •A-E
4 D-F•
5 A-B•
6 C-E•
7 F-G•
8 •B-E
9 A-C•
10 •D-E
11 B-F•
12 •A-G
13 C-D•
14 •E-F
15 B-G•
16 •A-D
17 •C-F
18 •E-G
19 •B-D
20 A-F•
21 C-G•

Two Playing Areas

PA I	PA II
1 A-B	
2 C-D	3 E-F
4 D-G	5 C-E
6 B-F	7 A-G
8 D-E	9 B-C
10 F-G	11 A-D
12 A-C	13 B-E
14 D-F	15 B-G
16 E-G	17 C-F
18 A-E	19 B-D
20 C-G	21 A-F

Three Playing Areas

PA I	PA II	PA III
1 C-E	2 A-G	3 B-F
4 A-C	5 B-E	6 D-G
7 F-G	8 D-E	9 B-C
10 E-G	11 C-F	12 A-D
13 A-B	14 C-D	15 E-F
16 D-F	17 B-G	18 A-E
19 B-D	20 A-F	21 C-G

EIGHT ENTRIES

One Playing Area

PA I
1 •F-H
2 •B-C
3 •A-E
4 •D-G
5 B-H•
6 •C-F
7 D-E•
8 A-G•
9 •D-H
10 •A-C
11 •B-E
12 •F-G
13 A-H•
14 B-G•
15 •C-D
16 •E-F
17 •A-B
18 •D-F
19 C-E•
20 •G-H
21 •B-D
22 A-F•
23 E-H•
24 •C-G
25 •A-D
26 •B-F
27 C-H•
28 E-G•

Two Playing Areas

PA I	PA II
1 A-B	2 C-D
3 E-F	4 G-H
5 B-E	6 A-C
7 D-G	8 F-H
9 C-G	10 A-E
11 B-H	12 D-F
13 E-H	14 A-G
15 C-F	16 B-D
17 A-H	18 F-G
19 D-E	20 B-C
21 A-F	22 D-H
23 B-G	24 C-E
25 A-D	26 B-F
27 C-H	28 E-G

Three Playing Areas

PA I	PA II	PA III
1 A-B		
4 E-F	2 C-D	3 G-H
7 D-E	5 F-G	6 A-H
10 D-H	8 B-C	9 A-F
13 D-G	11 A-C	12 B-E
16 A-E	14 F-H	15 C-G
19 C-F	17 E-H	18 B-D
22 A-G	20 B-H	21 D-F
25 B-G	23 A-D	24 C-E
28 C-H	26 E-G	27 B-F

PLAYING SCHEDULES
FOR ROUND ROBIN TOURNAMENTS

Four Playing Areas

PA I	PA II	PA III	PA IV
1 G-H	2 A-B	3 E-F	4 C-D
5 F-H	6 D-G	7 A-C	8 B-E
9 C-G	10 A-E	11 B-H	12 D-F
13 B-D	14 C-F	15 A-G	16 E-H
17 B-C	18 F-G	19 D-E	20 A-H
21 C-E	22 D-H	23 B-G	24 A-F
25 A-D	26 B-F	27 C-H	28 E-G

NINE ENTRIES

Two Playing Areas

PA I	PA II
1 •G-I	2 E-H•
3 •C-F	4 •A-D
5 •B-G	6 A-E•
7 •F-H	8 •D-I
9 •A-B	10 •C-D
11 •E-F	12 G-H•
13 A-I•	14 C-G•
15 •D-F	16 •B-H
17 C-E•	18 •A-G
19 B-I•	20 •D-H
21 D-G•	22 •F-I
23 A-C•	24 •B-E
25 •H-I	26 •F-G
27 D-E•	28 B-C•
29 •A-H	30 •B-F
31 E-G•	32 C-I•
33 •B-D	34 A-F•
35 C-H•	36 E-I•

Three Playing Areas

PA I	PA II	PA III
1 G-H	2 A-C	3 B-E
4 C-F	5 A-D	6 H-I
7 F-H	8 B-G	9 D-I
10 B-C	11 D-E	12 F-G
13 E-G	14 A-H	15 C-I
16 A-B	17 E-F	18 C-D
19 D-H	20 B-I	21 A-G
22 B-F	23 G-I	24 E-H
25 D-G	26 F-I	27 C-E
28 A-E	29 D-F	30 B-H
31 A-I	32 C-G	33 B-D
34 E-I	35 C-H	36 A-F

Four Playing Areas

PA I	PA II	PA III	PA IV
1 A-B	2 C-D	3 E-F	4 G-H
5 A-C	6 B-E	7 D-G	8 F-I
9 C-E	10 A-G	11 B-I	12 D-H
13 E-G	14 C-I	15 A-H	16 B-F
17 G-I	18 E-H	19 C-F	20 A-D
21 H-I	22 F-G	23 D-E	24 B-C
25 F-H	26 D-I	27 B-G	28 A-E
29 D-F	30 B-H	31 A-I	32 C-G
33 B-D	34 A-F	35 C-H	36 E-I

TEN ENTRIES

Three Playing Areas

PA I	PA II	PA III
1 C-E	2 B-G	3 A-F
4 D-F	5 B-H	6 A-I
7 A-G	8 E-I	9 C-J
10 B-I	11 D-J	12 F-H
13 F-G	14 B-C	15 D-E
16 I-J	17 G-H	18 A-C
19 A-H	20 F-J	21 D-I
22 A-B	23 C-D	24 E-F
25 C-F	26 E-H	27 G-J
28 B-D	29 A-J	30 H-I
31 B-E	32 F-I	33 D-G
34 H-J	35 A-E	36 C-G
37 D-H	38 C-I	39 B-J
40 E-G	41 A-D	42 B-F
43 C-H	44 G-I	45 E-J

Note: • = indicates home team for league play
– = indicates new round for league play

(continued)

PLAYING SCHEDULES

FOR ROUND ROBIN TOURNAMENTS

Four Playing Areas

PA I	PA II	PA III	PA IV
1 A-B			
2 I-J	3 C-D	4 G-H	5 E-F
6 E-I	7 D-J	8 F-H	9 A-G
10 D-F	11 A-I	12 B-H	13 C-J
14 D-G	15 B-E	16 A-C	17 F-I
18 C-F	19 G-J	20 B-D	21 E-H
22 A-E	23 H-J	24 C-G	25 B-I
26 H-I	27 F-G	28 D-E	29 A-J
30 F-J	31 A-H	32 D-I	33 B-C
34 B-G	35 C-E	36 A-F	37 D-H
38 E-G	39 C-I	40 B-J	41 A-D
42 C-H	43 B-F	44 E-J	45 G-I

Five Playing Areas

PA I	PA II	PA III	PA IV	PA V
1 •I-J	2 A-B•	3 E-F•	4 •G-H	5 •C-D
6 B-E•	7 F-I•	8 •D-G	9 •A-C	10 •H-J
11 •C-G	12 •D-J	13 B-I•	14 •A-E	15 F-H•
16 D-F•	17 A-G•	18 C-J•	19 •B-H	20 •E-I
21 •C-F	22 •G-J	23 E-H•	24 B-D•	25 •A-I
26 D-E•	27 H-I•	28 A-J•	29 •F-G	30 •B-C
31 •A-H	32 •C-E	33 B-G•	34 •D-I	35 F-J•
36 •B-J	37 D-H•	38 A-F•	39 C-I•	40•E-G
41 •G-I	42 •B-F	43 •C-H	44 E-J•	45 •A-D

PLAYING SCHEDULES
FOR ROUND ROBIN TOURNAMENTS

11 ENTRIES

Three Playing Areas

PA I	PA II	PA III
1 J-K		
2 A-B	3 C-F	4 D-G
5 D-E	6 F-G	7 H-I
8 A-K	9 B-J	10 C-I
11 G-H	12 A-D	13 E-F
14 C-D	15 H-K	16 F-I
17 A-C	18 I-J	19 B-E
20 B-K	21 F-H	22 D-J
23 D-I	24 A-E	25 B-G
26 E-H	27 G-J	28 I-K
29 B-F	30 C-J	31 A-H
32 D-F	33 A-I	34 C-G
35 G-I	36 D-H	37 E-K
38 H-J	39 B-C	40 F-K
41 B-I	42 C-E	43 A-G
44 E-G	45 D-K	46 F-J
47 C-K	48 B-H	49 A-J
50 A-F	51 E-I	52 B-D
53 E-J	54 G-K	55 C-H

Four Playing Areas

PA I	PA II	PA III	PA IV
1 C-D	2 A-B	3 E-F	
4 E-K	5 D-H	6 G-I	7 C-J
8 H-J	9 F-K	10 B-G	11 D-I
12 C-G	13 D-F	14 B-H	15 A-I
16 C-I	17 E-G	18 B-J	19 A-K
20 F-H	21 B-K	22 D-J	23 A-E
24 D-G	25 C-E	26 H-K	27 F-I
28 B-E	29 I-J	30 A-C	31 G-H
32 B-F	33 A-H	34 I-K	35 G-J
36 D-K	37 B-I	38 A-G	39 F-J
40 J-K	41 A-D	42 C-F	43 E-H
44 H-I	45 F-G	46 D-E	47 B-C
48 A-J	49 C-K	50 E-I	51 B-D
52 A-F	53 E-J	54 C-H	55 G-K

Note: • = indicates home team for league play
– = indicates new round for league play

(continued)

PLAYING SCHEDULES
FOR ROUND ROBIN TOURNAMENTS

Five Playing Areas

PA I	PA II	PA III	PA IV	PA V
1 •A-B	2 C-D•	3 •E-F	4 G-H•	5 •I-J
6 A-C•	7 •B-E	8 D-G•	9 •F-I	10 H-K•
11 C-E•	12 •A-G	13 B-I•	14 •D-K	15 F-J•
16 E-G•	17 •C-I	18 A-K•	19 •B-J	20 D-H•
21 G-I•	22 •E-K	23 C-J•	24 •A-H	25 B-F•
26 I-K•	27 •G-J	28 E-H•	29 C-F•	30 A-D•
31 •J-K	32 H-I•	33 •F-G	34 D-E•	35 •B-C
36 •H-J	37 F-K•	38 •D-I	39 B-G•	40 •A-E
41 •F-H	42 D-J•	43 •B-K	44 A-I•	45 •C-G
46 •D-F	47 B-H•	48 •A-J	49 C-K•	50 •E-I
51 •B-D	52 A-F•	53 •C-H	54 E-J•	55 •G-K

12 ENTRIES

Four Playing Area

PA I	PA II	PA III	PA IV
1 A-B	2 E-F		
3 G-H	4 I-J	5 C-D	6 K-L
7 C-E	8 A-H	9 B-G	10 F-J
11 F-I	12 D-G	13 B-E	14 A-C
15 F-L	16 D-K	17 B-I	18 H-J
19 A-K	20 I-L	21 G-J	22 E-H
23 B-D	24 A-L	25 C-F	26 J-K
27 F-G	28 D-E	29 H-I	30 B-C
31 H-L	32 F-K	33 A-J	34 D-I
35 E-I	36 C-K	37 A-G	38 B-L
39 C-J	40 B-H	41 E-L	42 D-F
43 G-K	44 A-I	45 D-J	46 F-H
47 B-K	48 C-I	49 D-L	50 E-G
51 J-L	52 C-G	53 H-K	54 A-E
55 D-H	56 B-J	57 A-F	58 C-L
59 A-D	60 B-F	61 E-K	62 G-I
63 E-J	64 G-L	65 C-H	66 I-K

PLAYING SCHEDULES

FOR ROUND ROBIN TOURNAMENTS

Five Playing Areas

PA I	PA II	PA III	PA IV	PA V
1 A-B				
2 E-F	3 C-D	4 I-J	5 G-H	6 K-L
7 H-K	8 F-I	9 A-C	10 B-E	11 D-G
12 A-E	13 J-L	14 D-K	15 B-I	16 C-G
17 C-K	18 A-G	19 F-L	20 H-J	21 E-I
22 B-L	23 D-J	24 F-H	25 G-K	26 A-I
27 D-F	28 E-L	29 B-H	30 C-J	31 A-K
32 G-J	33 C-F	34 E-H	35 I-L	36 B-D
37 J-K	38 F-G	39 A-L	40 D-E	41 H-I
42 H-L	43 D-I	44 A-J	45 F-K	46 B-C
47 D-L	48 A-H	49 B-G	50 C-E	51 F-J
52 C-I	53 B-K	54 E-G	55 A-F	56 D-H
57 G-I	58 E-K	59 B-J	60 A-D	61 C-L
62 B-F	63 C-H	64 I-K	65 G-L	66 E-J

Six Playing Areas

PA I	PA II	PA III	PA IV	PA V	PA VI
1 •K-L	2 •C-D	3 E-F•	4 •G-H	5 I-J•	6 A-B•
7 •A-C	8 B-E•	9 •D-G	10 F-I•	11 •H-K	12 J-L•
13 •A-E	14 F-L•	15 B-I•	16 •D-K	17 •C-G	18 •H-J
19 •E-I	20 A-G•	21 C-K•	22 •B-L	23 D-J•	24 •F-H
25 G-K•	26 A-I•	27 •B-H	28 C-J•	29 •E-L	30 D-F•
31 B-D•	32 •G-J	33 •A-K	34 E-H•	35 •C-F	36 I-L•
37 •J-K	38 H-I•	39 •F-G	40 A-L•	41 D-E•	42 •B-C
43 •H-L	44 F-K•	45 •D-I	46 B-G•	47 •A-J	48 •C-E
49 •F-J	50 D-L•	51 A-H•	52 C-I•	53 •B-K	54 •E-G
55 •G-I	56 B-J•	57 •C-L	58 E-K•	59 •A-F	60 •D-H
61 •B-F	62 C-H•	63 •E-J	64 •A-D	65 •G-L	66 •I-K

Note: • = indicates home team for league play
– = indicates new round for league play

(continued)

PLAYING SCHEDULES

FOR ROUND ROBIN TOURNAMENTS

13 ENTRIES

Four Playing Areas

PA I	PA II	PA III	PA IV
1 A-B	2 C-D		
3 K-L	4 G-H	5 E-F	6 I-J
7 D-E	8 B-C	9 H-M	10 J-L
11 A-H	12 I-L	13 K-M	14 B-F
15 D-L	16 F-J	17 G-I	18 E-K
19 H-K	20 J-M	21 C-E	22 A-G
23 C-G	24 A-I	25 D-J	26 F-H
27 B-I	28 D-K	29 F-M	30 H-L
31 E-G	32 C-I	33 A-K	34 B-M
35 G-J	36 E-H	37 C-F	38 A-D
39 H-J	40 F-L	41 B-K	42 D-M
43 C-K	44 A-M	45 B-L	46 E-I
47 A-C	48 B-E	49 F-I	50 D-G
51 L-M	52 F-G	53 H-I	54 J-K
55 B-J	56 A-L	57 D-H	58 C-M
59 F-K	60 D-I	61 A-E	62 B-G
63 E-L	64 G-M	65 C-J	66 I-K
67 D-F	68 B-H	69 A-J	70 C-L
71 E-M	72 G-K	73 B-D	74 A-F
75 I-M	76 E-J	77 G-L	78 C-H

Five Playing Areas

PA I	PA II	PA III	PA IV	PA V
1 A-B	2 C-D	3 E-F		
4 I-J	5 G-H	6 K-L	7 A-C	8 B-E
9 B-K	10 F-L	11 H-J	12 A-E	13 D-M
14 D-G	15 J-M	16 H-K	17 F-I	18 C-E
19 C-I	20 A-K	21 E-G	22 D-L	23 B-M
24 K-M	25 B-F	26 A-H	27 C-J	28 I-L
29 F-G	30 H-I	31 B-C	32 D-E	33 J-K
34 E-H	35 C-F	36 A-D	37 L-M	38 G-J
39 E-L	40 G-M	41 I-K	42 B-J	43 D-H
44 B-I	45 A-G	46 F-M	47 D-K	48 H-L
49 A-L	50 E-K	51 C-M	52 F-J	53 G-I
54 J-L	55 D-I	56 B-G	57 H-M	58 F-K
59 D-F	60 A-M	61 E-I	62 B-H	63 C-K
64 F-H	65 B-L	66 D-J	67 C-G	68 A-I
69 E-M	70 B-D	71 C-L	72 G-K	73 A-J
74 C-H	75 E-J	76 G-L	77 I-M	78 A-F

PLAYING SCHEDULES
FOR ROUND ROBIN TOURNAMENTS

Six Playing Areas

PA I	PA II	PA III	PA IV	PA V	PA VI
1 A-B•	2 •C-D	3 E-F•	4 •G-H	5 I-J•	6 •K-L
7 •A-C	8 B-E•	9 •D-G	10 F-I•	11 •H-K	12 J-M•
13 •C-E	14 A-G•	15 •B-I	16 D-K•	17 •F-M	18 H-L•
19 •E-G	20 C-I•	21 •A-K	22 B-M•	23 •D-L	24 F-J•
25 •G-I	26 E-K•	27 •C-M	28 A-L•	29 •B-J	30 D-H•
31 •I-K	32 G-M•	33 •E-L	34 C-J•	35 •A-H	36 •B-F
37 •K-M	38 I-L•	39 •G-J	40 E-H•	41 •C-F	42 A-D•
43 L-M•	44 •J-K	45 H-I•	46 •F-G	47 D-E•	48 •B-C
49 J-L•	50 •H-M	51 F-K•	52 •D-I	53 B-G•	54 •A-E
55 H-J•	56 •F-L	57 D-M•	58 •B-K	59 A-I•	60 •C-G
61 F-H•	62 •D-J	63 B-L•	64 •A-M	65 C-K•	66 •E-I
67 D-F•	68 •B-H	69 A-J•	70 •C-L	71 E-M•	72 •G-K
73 B-D•	74 •A-F	75 C-H•	76 •E-J	77 G-L•	78 •I-M

14 ENTRIES

Five Playing Areas

PA I	PA II	PA III	PA IV	PA V
1 A-B				
2 E-H	3 C-F	4 B-D	5 A-N	6 L-M
7 D-M	8 B-K	9 C-I	10 E-G	11 A-H
12 D-F	13 A-M	14 K-N	15 I-L	16 G-J
17 J-K	18 H-I	19 F-G	20 D-E	21 B-C
22 B-G	23 C-E	24 A-J	25 H-L	26 F-N
27 A-L	28 J-N	29 H-M	30 F-K	31 D-I
32 A-G	33 E-I	34 C-K	35 B-M	36 D-N
37 F-L	38 H-J	39 A-I	40 G-K	41 E-M
42 I-M	43 G-N	44 E-L	45 C-J	46 B-H
47 C-N	48 B-L	49 D-J	50 F-H	51 A-K
52 M-N	53 A-C	54 B-E	55 D-G	56 F-I
57 C-D	58 E-F	59 G-H	60 K-L	61 I-J
62 B-I	63 D-K	64 F-M	65 H-N	66 J-L
67 H-K	68 J-M	69 L-N	70 A-E	71 C-G
72 E-N	73 G-M	74 I-K	75 A-D	76 B-F
77 G-I	78 A-F	79 D-H	80 B-J	81 C-L
82 F-J	83 D-L	84 B-N	85 C-M	86 E-K
87 C-H	88 G-L	89 E-J	90 I-N	91 K-M

Note: • = indicates home team for league play
    – = indicates new round for league play

(continued)

PLAYING SCHEDULES

FOR ROUND ROBIN TOURNAMENTS

Six Playing Areas

PA I	PA II	PA III	PA IV	PA V	PA VI
1 K-L					
2 A-B	3 C-D	4 E-F	5 I-J	6 G-H	7 M-N
8 F-I	9 J-M	10 H-K	11 B-E	12 D-G	13 A-C
14 C-G	15 B-I	16 A-E	17 D-K	18 L-N	19 F-M
20 C-K	21 H-N	22 A-G	23 E-I	24 J-L	25 B-M
26 H-J	27 G-K	28 D-N	29 F-L	30 E-M	31 A-I
32 I-M	33 F-H	34 B-L	35 C-N	36 A-K	37 D-J
38 D-F	39 E-L	40 G-N	41 A-M	42 C-J	43 B-H
44 B-D	45 K-N	46 I-L	47 C-F	48 E-H	49 G-J
50 A-N	51 H-I	52 J-K	53 D-E	54 L-M	55 F-G
56 H-M	57 A-L	58 B-C	59 J-N	60 D-I	61 F-K
62 A-J	63 B-G	64 D-M	65 H-L	66 F-N	67 C-E
68 E-G	69 D-L	70 F-J	71 A-H	72 C-I	73 B-K
74 E-K	75 C-M	76 G-I	77 B-N	78 A-F	79 D-H
80 E-N	81 A-D	82 I-K	83 G-M	84 B-J	85 C-L
86 G-L	87 E-J	88 C-H	89 K-M	90 B-F	91 I-N

Seven Playing Areas

PA I	PA II	PA III	PA IV	PA V	PA VI	PA VII
1 •A-B	2 C-D•	3 •E-F	4 G-H•	5 K-L•	6 •I-J	7 •M-N
8 A-C•	9 •B-E	10 D-G•	11 •F-I	12 H-K•	13 •J-M	14 L-N•
15 •C-G	16 •A-E	17 B-I•	18 •D-K	19 F-M•	20 •H-N	21 J-L•
22 •E-I	23 C-K•	24 A-G•	25 •B-M	26 D-N•	27 •F-L	28 H-J•
29 •G-K	30 E-M•	31 •C-N	32 •D-J	33 B-L•	34 •A-I	35 F-H•
36 •I-M	37 G-N•	38 A-K•	39 •E-L	40 C-J•	41 •B-H	42 D-F•
43 •K-N	44 I-L•	45 •A-M	46 •G-J	47 E-H•	48 •C-F	49 B-D•
50 L-M•	51 •J-K	52 H-I•	53 A-N•	54 •F-G	55 D-E•	56 •B-C
57 J-N•	58 •H-M	59 F-K•	60 •A-L	61 •D-I	62 B-G•	63 •C-E
64 H-L•	65 •F-N	66 D-M•	67 •B-K	68 A-J•	69 C-I•	70 •E-G
71 F-J•	72 •D-L	73 B-N•	74 •C-M	75 •A-H	76 E-K•	77 •G-I
78 D-H•	79 •B-J	70 C-L•	81 •E-N	82 G-M•	83 A-F•	84 •I-K
85 B-F•	86 •C-H	87 E-J•	88 •K-M	89 I-N•	90 •G-L	91 •A-D

PLAYING SCHEDULES

FOR ROUND ROBIN TOURNAMENTS

15 ENTRIES

Six Playing Areas

PA I		PA II		PA III		PA IV		PA V		PA VI	
1	C-D	2	A-B	3	E-F						
4	B-E	5	A-C	6	G-H	7	M-N	8	K-L	9	I-J
10	J-M	11	L-O	12	C-E	13	D-G	14	F-I	15	H-K
16	D-K	17	H-O	18	J-N	19	B-I	20	A-G	21	F-M
22	A-K	23	F-N	24	D-O	25	E-G	26	C-I	27	B-M
28	C-M	29	G-I	30	B-N	31	E-K	32	H-L	33	A-O
34	E-O	35	G-M	36	I-K	37	D-L	38	F-J	39	C-N
40	I-O	41	K-M	42	A-L	43	B-J	44	G-N	45	D-H
46	B-F	47	E-L	48	K-N	49	A-H	50	M-O	51	C-J
52	I-L	53	E-H	54	C-F	55	G-J	56	N-O	57	A-D
58	F-G	59	D-E	60	L-M	61	H-I	62	J-K	63	B-C
64	H-M	65	J-O	66	B-G	67	F-K	68	D-I	69	L-N
70	J-L	71	B-K	72	D-M	73	F-O	74	A-E	75	H-N
76	H-J	77	C-G	78	A-I	79	D-N	80	B-O	81	F-L
82	C-K	83	D-J	84	F-H	85	A-M	86	B-L	87	E-I
88	A-N	89	D-F	90	B-H	91	C-O	92	E-M	93	G-K
94	E-N	95	I-M	96	A-J	97	C-L	98	B-D	99	G-O
100	G-L	101	I-N	102	K-O	103	A-F	104	C-H	105	E-J

Seven Playing Areas

PA I		PA II		PA III		PA IV		PA V		PA VI		PA VII	
1	•A-B	2	C-D•	3	•E-F	4	G-H•	5	•I-J	6	K-L•	7	M-N•
8	A-C•	9	•B-E	10	D-G•	11	•F-I	12	H-K•	13	•J-M	14	L-O•
15	C-E•	16	•A-G	17	B-I•	18	•D-K	19	F-M•	20	•H-O	21	J-N•
22	E-G•	23	•C-I	24	A-K•	25	•B-M	26	D-O•	27	•F-N	28	H-L•
29	G-I•	30	•E-K	31	C-M•	32	•A-O	33	B-N•	34	•D-L	35	F-J•
36	I-K•	37	•G-M	38	E-O•	39	•C-N	40	A-L•	41	•B-J	42	D-H•
43	K-M•	44	•I-O	45	G-N•	46	•E-L	47	C-J•	48	•A-H	49	B-F•
50	M-O•	51	•K-N	52	I-L•	53	•G-J	54	E-H•	55	•C-F	56	A-D•
57	•N-O	58	L-M•	59	•J-K	60	H-I•	61	•F-G	62	D-E•	63	•B-C
64	•L-N	65	J-O•	66	•H-M	67	F-K•	68	•D-I	69	B-G•	70	•A-E
71	•J-L	72	H-N•	73	•F-O	74	D-M•	75	•B-K	76	A-I•	77	•C-G
78	•H-J	79	•F-L	80	•D-N	81	B-O•	82	•A-M	83	C-K•	84	•E-I
85	•F-H	86	D-J•	87	•B-L	88	A-N•	89	•C-O	90	E-M•	91	•G-K
92	•D-F	93	B-H•	94	•A-J	95	C-L•	96	•E-N	97	G-O•	98	I-M•
99	•B-D	100	A-F•	101	•C-H	102	E-J•	103	G-L•	104	•I-N	105	•K-O

Note: • = indicates home team for league play
– = indicates new round for league play

(continued)

16 ENTRIES

Seven Playing Areas

PA I	PA II	PA III	PA IV	PA V	PA VI	PA VII
1 A-B						
2 O-P	3 M-M	4 I-J	5 C-D	6 E-F	7 K-L	8 G-H
9 L-O	10 A-C	11 F-I	12 H-K	13 B-E	14 D-G	15 J-M
16 N-P	17 H-O	18 A-E	19 B-I	20 F-M	21 D-K	22 C-G
23 D-O	24 E-I	25 B-M	26 A-G	27 J-P	28 C-K	29 L-N
30 H-N	31 G-K	32 E-M	33 F-P	34 C-O	35 A-I	36 J-L
37 F-L	38 D-N	39 H-J	40 G-O	41 A-K	42 B-P	43 I-M
44 E-P	45 F-H	46 K-O	47 D-J	48 B-L	49 C-N	50 A-M
51 B-H	52 I-P	53 G-N	54 C-J	55 D-F	56 A-O	57 E-L
58 G-J	59 K-N	60 I-L	61 B-D	62 M-P	63 E-H	64 C-F
65 F-G	66 A-P	67 N-O	68 H-I	69 J-K	70 L-M	71 D-E
72 B-C	73 J-O	74 F-K	75 L-P	76 A-N	77 H-M	78 D-I
79 D-M	80 C-E	81 B-G	82 A-L	83 J-N	84 F-O	85 H-P
86 A-J	87 H-L	88 D-P	89 F-N	90 C-I	91 E-G	92 B-K
93 C-M	94 D-L	95 A-H	96 E-K	97 G-I	98 F-J	99 B-O
100 I-K	101 G-M	102 C-P	103 E-O	104 D-H	105 B-N	106 A-F
107 A-D	108 B-J	109 C-L	110 K-M	111 I-O	112 G-P	113 E-N
114 E-J	115 B-F	116 C-H	117 M-O	118 G-L	119 I-N	120 K-P

Eight Playing Areas

PA I	PA II	PA III	PA IV	PA V	PA VI	PA VII	PA VIII
1 •A-B	2 C-D•	3 G-H•	4 •I-J	5 •E-F	6 K-L•	7 •M-N	8 O-P•
9 •B-E	10 H-K•	11 •J-M	12 D-G•	13 A-C•	14 •F-I	15 L-O•	16 •N-P
17 •C-G	18 B-I•	19 •D-K	20 F-M•	21 •H-O	22 J-P•	23 •A-E	24 •L-N
25 C-K•	26 •E-I	27 •B-M	28 H-N•	29 •F-P	30 D-O•	31 •J-L	32 A-G•
33 •G-K	34 E-M•	35 •C-O	36 F-L•	37 •D-N	38 B-P•	39 •A-I	40 •H-J
41 •I-M	42 G-O•	43 •E-P	44 A-K•	45 •B-L	46 D-J•	47 C-N•	48 •F-H
49 •K-O	50 •A-M	51 I-P•	52 •G-N	53 •C-J	54 E-L•	55 B-H•	56 •D-F
57 •M-P	58 G-J•	59 •I-L	60 •E-H	61 K-N•	62 A-O•	63 C-F•	64 •B-D
65 •O-N	66 •A-P	67 J-K•	68 B-C•	69 •H-I	70 F-G•	71 •D-E	72 •L-M
73 L-P•	74 •J-O	75 A-N•	76 D-I•	77 •B-G	78 H-M•	79 •F-K	80 C-E•
81 J-N•	82 •H-P	83 F-O•	84 •A-L	85 •D-M	86 B-K•	87 •C-I	88 E-G•
89 H-L•	90 •F-N	91 •E-K	92 •B-O	93 G-I•	94 C-M•	95 D-P•	96 A-J•
97 F-J•	98 •D-L	99 B-N•	100 •C-P	101 E-O•	102 •A-H	103 •G-M	104 I-K•
105 D-H•	106 C-L•	107 A-F•	108 G-P•	109 K-M•	110 •E-N	111 •B-J	112 •I-O
113 •A-D	114 •B-F	115 •C-H	116 E-J•	117 •K-P	118 •I-N	119 •G-L	120 M-O•

FOR ROUND ROBIN—DOUBLE SPLIT TOURNAMENTS

SIX ENTRIES

Two Playing Areas

POOL 1	POOL 2
PA I	PA II
1 A-B	2 A-B
3 B-C	4 B-C
5 A-C	6 A-C

SEVEN ENTRIES

Two Playing Areas

POOL 1		POOL 2
PA I	PA II	PA II
1 A-C		
2 B-D		3 A-B
4 B-C	5 A-D	
6 A-B		7 B-C
8 C-D		9 A-C

Three Playing Areas

POOL 1		POOL 2
PA I	PA II	PA III
1 A-B	2 A-C	3 B-D
4 B-C	5 A-D	6 B-C
7 A-C	8 C-D	9 A-B

EIGHT ENTRIES

Two Playing Areas

POOL 1	POOL 2
PA I	PA II
1 A-C	2 A-C
3 B-D	4 B-D
5 A-D	6 A-D
7 B-C	8 B-C
9 A-B	10 A-B
11 C-D	12 C-D

Three Playing Areas

POOL 1		POOL 2	
PA I	PA II	PA III	PA IV
1 A-C	2 B-D		3 A-C
4 A-D	5 B-C		6 B-D
7 A-B		8 A-D	9 B-C
10 C-D		11 A-B	12 C-D

Four Playing Areas

POOL 1		POOL 2	
PA I	PA II	PA III	PA IV
1 A-C	2 B-D	3 A-C	4 B-D
5 A-D	6 B-C	7 A-D	8 B-C
9 C-D	10 A-B	11 C-D	12 A-B

NINE ENTRIES

Two Playing Areas

POOL 1	POOL 2	
PA I	PA I	PA II
	1 A-D	2 B-C
3 A-C		4 D-E
5 B-D		6 A-C
7 A-D		8 B-E
	9 C-D	10 A-B
11 B-C		12 C-E
13 A-B		14 B-D
15 C-D		16 A-E

Three Playing Areas

POOL 1		POOL 2
PA I	PA II	PA III
1 A-C		
2 B-D	3 C-E	4 A-D
5 A-D	6 A-C	7 B-E
8 B-C	9 A-B	10 C-D
11 A-B	12 D-E	13 B-C
14 C-D	15 B-D	16 A-E

(continued)

PLAYING SCHEDULES

FOR ROUND ROBIN—DOUBLE SPLIT TOURNAMENTS

Four Playing Areas

POOL 1		POOL 2	
PA I	PA II	PA III	PA IV
1 A-C	2 B-D	3 C-E	4 A-D
		5 A-C	6 B-E
7 A-D	8 B-C	9 A-B	10 C-D
		11 D-E	12 B-C
13 A-B	14 C-D	15 B-D	16 A-E

10 ENTRIES

Two Playing Areas

POOL 1	POOL 2
PA I	PA II
1 A-D	2 A-D
3 B-C	4 B-C
5 D-E	6 D-E
7 A-C	8 A-C
9 B-E	10 B-E
11 C-D	12 C-D
13 A-B	14 A-B
15 C-E	16 C-E
17 B-D	18 B-D
19 A-E	20 A-E

Three Playing Areas

POOL 1		POOL 2	
PA I	PA II	PA II	PA III
1 B-C	2 A-D		
3 D-E		4 C-E	5 A-D
6 A-C	7 B-E		8 B-E
9 A-B	10 C-D		11 A-C
12 C-E		13 A-B	14 C-D
15 B-D		16 D-E	17 B-C
18 A-E		19 B-D	20 A-E

Four Playing Areas

POOL 1		POOL 2	
PA I	PA II	PA III	PA IV
1 C-E	2 A-D	3 C-E	4 A-D
5 A-C	6 B-E	7 A-C	8 B-E
9 A-B	10 C-D	11 A-B	12 C-D
13 D-E	14 B-C	15 D-E	16 B-C
17 B-D	18 A-E	19 B-D	20 A-E

11 ENTRIES

Two Playing Areas

POOL 1		POOL 2
PA I	PA II	PA II
1 C-D		
2 E-F	3 A-B	
4 A-C		5 A-D
6 B-E		7 B-C
8 D-F		9 D-E
10 A-E		11 A-C
12 B-D	13 C-F	
14 A-F		15 B-E
16 D-E		17 C-D
18 B-C		19 A-B
20 A-D		21 C-E
22 B-F		23 B-D
24 C-E		25 A-E

Three Playing Areas

POOL 1		POOL 2	
PA I	PA II	PA II	PA III
1 A-B			
2 E-F	3 C-D		4 A-D
5 A-C	6 B-E		7 B-C
8 D-F		9 A-C	10 D-E
11 C-F	12 A-E		13 B-E
14 B-D	15 A-F		16 C-D
17 D-E		18 C-E	19 A-B
20 A-D	21 B-C		22 B-D
23 C-E	24 B-F		25 A-E

PLAYING SCHEDULES

FOR ROUND ROBIN—DOUBLE SPLIT TOURNAMENTS

Four Playing Areas

POOL 1			POOL 2	
PA I	PA II	PA III	PA III	PA IV
1 C-D	2 E-F	3 A-B		
4 D-F	5 A-C		6 B-F	7 C-D
8 I-E	9 B-D		10 A-D	11 B-C
12 B-E	13 C-F		14 C-E	15 A-B
16 B-C	17 A-D		18 I-C	19 D-E
20 A-F	21 D-E		22 B-D	
23 B-F	24 C-E		25 A-E	

Five Playing Areas

POOL 1			POOL 2	
PA I	PA II	PA III	PA IV	PA V
1 C-E	2 A-D	3 A-B	4 E-F	5 C-D
6 A-C	7 B-E	8 D-F	9 A-C	10 B-E
11 A-B	12 C-D	13 A-E	14 B-D	15 C-F
16 B-E	17 B-E	18 B-C	19 D-E	20 A-F
21 B-D	22 A-E	23 C-E	24 B-F	25 A-D

12 ENTRIES

Two Playing Areas

POOL 1	POOL 2
PA I	PA II
1 A-B	2 A-B
3 C-D	4 C-D
5 E-F	6 E-F
7 A-C	8 A-C
9 B-E	10 B-E
11 D-F	12 D-F
13 A-E	14 A-E
15 C-F	16 C-F
17 B-D	18 B-D
19 A-F	20 A-F
21 D-E	22 D-E
23 B-C	24 B-C
25 A-D	26 A-D
27 B-F	28 B-F
29 C-E	30 C-E

Three Playing Areas

POOL 1		POOL 2	
PA I	PA II	PA II	PA III
1 C-D	2 A-B		3 A-B
4 E-F		5 C-D	6 E-F
7 B-E	8 A-C		9 A-C
10 D-F		11 B-E	12 D-F
13 A-E	14 C-F		15 A-E
16 B-D		17 C-F	18 B-D
19 A-F	20 D-E		21 A-F
22 B-C		23 D-E	24 B-C
25 A-D	26 B-F		27 A-D
28 C-E		29 B-F	30 C-E

(continued)

PLAYING SCHEDULES

FOR ROUND ROBIN—DOUBLE SPLIT TOURNAMENTS

Four Playing Areas

	POOL 1			POOL 2	
PA I		PA II	PA III		PA IV
1 A-B			2 A-B		
3 C-D		4 E-F	5 C-D		6 E-F
7 D-F		8 A-E	9 D-F		10 A-E
11 B-E		12 A-C	13 B-E		14 A-C
15 C-F		16 B-D	17 C-F		18 B-D
19 A-F		20 D-E	21 A-F		22 D-E
23 A-D		24 B-C	25 A-D		26 B-C
27 C-E		28 B-F	29 C-E		30 B-F

Five Playing Areas

	POOL 1				POOL 2	
PA I	PA II	PA III	PA III		PA IV	PA V
1 A-B	2 C-D	3 E-F			4 A-B	5 E-F
6 D-F	7 B-E	8 A-C			9 C-D	10 A-C
11 A-E	12 C-F	13 B-D			14 D-F	15 B-E
16 B-C	17 D-E		18 B-D		19 A-E	20 C-F
21 C-E	22 A-F		23 A-F		24 D-E	25 B-C
26 B-F	27 A-D		28 C-E		29 B-F	30 A-D

Six Playing Areas

	POOL 1			POOL 2	
PA I	PA II	PA III	PA IV	PA V	PA VI
1 A-B	2 E-F	3 C-D	4 A-B	5 E-F	6 C-D
7 D-F	8 A-C	9 B-E	10 D-F	11 A-C	12 B-E
13 A-E	14 B-D	15 C-F	16 A-E	17 B-D	18 C-F
19 B-C	20 D-E	21 A-F	22 B-C	23 D-E	24 A-F
25 C-E	26 B-F	27 A-D	28 C-E	29 B-F	30 A-D

PLAYING SCHEDULES
FOR ROUND ROBIN—DOUBLE SPLIT TOURNAMENTS

13 ENTRIES

Two Playing Areas

POOL 1		POOL 2	
PA I	PA I		PA II
	1 C-D		2 A-B
3 A-C			4 E-F
5 E-F			6 A-G
	7 B-E		8 C-F
9 C-D			10 D-G
11 A-B			12 A-E
	13 D-F		14 B-C
15 B-E			16 E-G
17 D-F			18 A-C
19 A-E			20 F-G
21 C-F			22 B-D
23 B-D			24 C-E
25 A-F			26 B-F
27 D-E			28 A-D
29 B-C			30 B-G
31 A-D			32 D-E
33 B-F			34 A-F
35 C-E			36 C-G

Three Playing Areas

POOL 1		POOL 2	
PA I	PA II	PA II	PA III
1 A-C		2 C-D	3 A-B
4 E-F		5 E-F	6 A-G
7 C-D	8 A-B		9 B-E
10 B-E		11 C-F	12 D-G
13 D-F		14 A-E	15 B-C
16 A-E	17 C-F		18 D-F
19 B-D		20 E-G	21 A-C
22 A-F		23 B-D	24 F-G
25 B-C	26 D-E		27 C-E
28 A-D		29 A-D	30 B-F
31 B-F		32 B-G	33 D-E
34 C-E		35 A-F	36 C-G

Four Playing Areas

POOL 1			POOL 2	
PA I	PA II	PA II	PA III	PA IV
1 A-B		2 A-B	3 E-F	4 C-D
5 C-D		6 C-F	7 A-G	8 B-E
9 E-F	10 A-C		11 D-G	12 A-E
13 D-F	14 B-E		15 B-C	16 D-F
17 A-E	18 C-F		19 B-D	20 A-C
21 B-D		22 E-G	23 C-E	24 F-G
25 A-F	26 D-E		27 A-D	28 B-F
29 B-C	30 A-D		31 B-G	32 D-E
33 C-E	34 B-F		35 A-F	36 C-G

(continued)

FOR ROUND ROBIN—DOUBLE SPLIT TOURNAMENTS

Five Playing Areas

POOL 1			POOL 2		
PA I	PA II	PA III	PA III	PA IV	PA V
			1 A-B		
2 A-B	3 C-D	4 E-F		5 C-D	6 E-F
7 A-C	8 B-E		9 A-C	10 B-E	11 D-G
12 D-F	13 A-E		14 C-E	15 A-G	16 B-F
17 C-F	18 B-D		19 E-G	20 C-F	21 A-D
22 A-F	23 D-E		24 F-G	25 D-E	26 B-C
27 B-C	28 A-D		29 D-F	30 B-G	31 A-E
32 C-E	33 B-F		34 B-D	35 A-F	36 C-G

Six Playing Areas

POOL 1			POOL 2		
PA I	PA II	PA III	PA IV	PA V	PA VI
1 A-B	2 C-D	3 E-F			
4 A-C	5 B-E	6 D-G			
7 C-3	8 A-G	9 B-F	10 A-B	11 E-F	12 C-D
13 E-G	14 C-F	15 A-D	16 D-F	17 A-C	18 B-E
19 F-G	20 D-E	21 B-C	22 A-E	23 B-D	24 C-F
25 D-F	26 B-G	27 A-E	28 B-C	29 D-E	30 A-F
31 B-D	33 A-F	33 C-G	34 C-E	35 B-F	36 A-D

Two Playing Areas

See Round Robin Seven Entries—One Playing Area

Three Playing Areas

POOL 1		POOL 2	
PA I	PA II	PA II	PA III
1 D-G	2 E-F		3 D-G
4 A-B		5 A-B	6 E-F
7 E-G	8 D-F		9 E-G
10 B-C		11 B-C	12 D-F
13 D-E	14 A-C		15 D-E
16 F-G		17 F-G	18 A-C
19 A-D	20 B-E		21 B-E
22 C-F		23 A-D	24 C-F
25 A-E	26 B-G		27 B-G
28 C-D		29 A-E	30 C-D
31 B-F	32 A-G		33 B-F
34 C-E		35 C-E	36 A-G
37 A-F	38 B-D		39 B-D
40 C-G		41 C-G	42 A-F

Four Playing Areas

POOL 1		POOL 2	
PA I	PA II	PA III	PA IV
1 A-B		2 A-B	
3 C-D	4 E-F	5 C-D	6 E-F
7 D-G	8 C-E	9 D-G	10 C-E
11 B-F	12 A-G	13 B-F	14 A-G
15 D-E	16 B-C	17 D-E	18 B-C
19 F-G	20 A-D	21 F-G	22 A-D
23 A-C	24 B-E	25 A-C	26 B-E
27 E-G	28 C-F	29 E-G	30 C-F
31 D-F	32 B-G	33 D-F	34 B-G
35 A-E	36 B-D	37 A-E	38 B-D
39 C-G	40 A-F	41 C-G	42 A-F

PLAYING SCHEDULES

FOR ROUND ROBIN—DOUBLE SPLIT TOURNAMENTS

Five Playing Areas

	POOL 1			POOL 2	
PA I	PA II	PA III	PA III	PA IV	PA V
1 C-D	2 A-B				
3 A-C	4 E-F		5 A-B	6 C-D	7 E-F
8 B-E	9 D-G		10 B-E	11 A-C	12 D-G
13 C-E	14 B-F	15 A-G		16 C-E	17 A-G
18 E-G	19 A-D	20 C-F		21 B-F	22 E-G
23 F-G	24 B-C	25 D-E		26 C-F	27 A-D
28 B-G	29 D-F		30 F-G	31 D-E	32 B-C
33 B-D	34 A-E		35 D-F	36 B-G	37 A-E
38 A-F	39 C-G		40 C-G	41 A-F	42 B-D

Six Playing Areas

	POOL 1			POOL 2	
PA I	PA II	PA III	PA IV	PA V	PA VI
1 A-B	2 C-D	3 E-F	4 A-B	5 C-D	6 E-F
7 A-C	8 B-E	9 D-G	10 A-C	11 B-E	12 D-G
13 C-E	14 A-G	15 B-F	16 C-E	17 A-G	18 B-F
19 E-G	20 C-F	21 A-D	22 E-G	23 C-F	24 A-D
25 F-G	26 D-E	27 B-C	28 F-G	29 D-E	30 B-C
31 D-F	32 B-G	33 A-E	34 D-F	35 B-G	36 A-E
37 B-D	38 A-F	39 C-G	40 B-D	41 A-F	42 C-G

(continued)

PLAYING SCHEDULES

FOR ROUND ROBIN—DOUBLE SPLIT TOURNAMENTS

15 ENTRIES

Two Playing Areas

POOL 1	POOL 2	
PA I	PA I	PA II
	1 A-B	
	2 C-D	3 E-F
4 A-B		5 G-H
	6 B-E	7 A-C
	8 F-H	9 D-G
10 D-G		11 A-E
12 E-F		13 B-H
14 A-C		15 C-G
16 E-G		17 D-F
17 D-F		19 A-G
20 B-C		21 E-H
22 D-E		23 C-F
24 F-G		25 B-D
26 B-E		27 A-H
28 A-D		29 F-G
30 C-F		31 D-E
32 B-G		33 B-C
34 A-E		35 A-F
36 C-D		37 D-H
38 B-F		39 B-G
40 A-G		41 C-E
42 C-E		43 A-D
44 B-D		45 B-F
46 A-F		47 C-H
48 C-G		49 E-G

Three Playing Areas

POOL 1		POOL 2	
PA I	PA II	PA II	PA III
1 A-B			
2 E-F	3 C-D		4 A-B
5 G-H		6 D-G	7 E-F
8 A-C	9 B-E		10 A-C
11 F-H	12 D-G		13 E-G
14 A-E		15 D-F	16 B-C
17 C-G	18 B-H		19 D-E
20 D-F	21 A-G		22 F-G
23 E-H		24 B-E	25 A-D
26 B-D	27 C-F		28 C-F
29 A-H	30 F-G		31 B-G
32 D-E		33 A-E	34 C-D
35 A-F	36 B-C		37 B-F
38 B-G	39 D-H		40 A-G
41 C-E		42 C-E	43 B-D
44 B-F	45 A-D		46 A-F
47 E-G	48 C-H		49 C-G

FOR ROUND ROBIN—DOUBLE SPLIT TOURNAMENTS

Four Playing Areas

	POOL 1			POOL 2	
PA I	PA II	PA III	PA III	PA IV	
1 A-B					
2 C-D	3 E-F		4 E-F	5 D-G	
6 G-H	7 A-C		8 A-B	9 E-G	
10 D-G	11 B-E	12 F-H		13 D-F	
14 A-E	15 C-G		16 D-E	17 B-C	
18 D-F	19 B-H		20 F-G	21 A-C	
22 E-H	23 C-F	24 A-G		25 B-E	
26 B-D	27 A-H		28 C-F	29 A-D	
30 F-G	31 D-E		32 A-E	33 B-G	
34 A-F	35 D-H	36 B-C		37 C-D	
38 C-E	39 B-G		40 A-G	41 B-F	
42 B-F	43 A-D		44 B-D	45 C-E	
46 C-H	47 E-G		48 C-G	49 A-F	

Five Playing Areas

	POOL 1			POOL 2	
PA I	PA II	PA III	PA III	PA IV	PA V
1 C-D	2 E-F	3 A-B		4 A-B	
5 D-G	6 C-E		7 C-D	8 E-F	9 G-H
10 B-F	11 A-G		12 F-G	13 D-E	14 A-H
15 D-E	16 B-C		17 B-C	18 D-H	19 A-F
20 F-G	21 A-D		22 A-C	23 D-G	24 B-E
25 A-C	26 B-E		27 F-H	28 A-E	29 C-G
30 D-F	31 B-G		32 A-H	33 C-F	34 B-D
35 E-G	36 C-F		37 B-H	38 A-G	39 D-F
40 A-E	41 B-D		42 A-D	43 B-G	44 C-E
45 C-G	46 A-F		47 E-G	48 C-H	49 B-F

Six Playing Areas

	POOL 1			POOL 2		
PA I	PA II	PA III	PA III	PA IV	PA V	PA VI
1 D-G	2 E-F					
3 A-B			4 G-H	5 A-B	6 E-F	7 C-D
9 D-F	8 E-G		10 F-H	11 D-G	12 A-C	13 B-E
15 B-C	14 D-E		16 A-E	17 B-H	18 C-G	19 D-F
21 F-G	20 A-C		22 B-D	23 C-F	24 A-G	25 E-H
27 B-E	26 A-D	28 C-F		29 A-H	30 D-E	31 B-C
33 C-D	32 B-G	34 A-E		35 C-E	36 D-H	37 F-G
39 C-E	38 B-F	40 A-G		41 B-G	42 C-H	43 A-F
45 A-F	44 C-G	46 B-D		47 A-D	48 B -F	49 E-G

(continued)

PLAYING SCHEDULES

FOR ROUND ROBIN—DOUBLE SPLIT TOURNAMENTS

Seven Playing Areas

	POOL 1				POOL 2	
PA I	PA II	PA III	PA IV	PA V	PA VI	PA VII
1 A-B	2 C-D	3 E-F	4 G-H	5 A-B	6 E-F	7 C-D
8 A-C	9 B-E	10 D-G	11 F-H	12 D-G	13 A-C	14 B-E
15 C-E	16 A-G	17 B-F	18 C-G	19 A-E	20 B-H	21 D-F
22 E-G	23 C-F	24 A-D	25 B-D	26 C-F	27 A-G	28 E-H
29 F-G	30 D-E	31 B-C	32 B-C	33 F-G	34 D-E	35 A-H
36 D-F	37 B-G	38 A-E	39 C-E	40 D-H	41 B-G	42 A-F
43 B-D	44 A-F	45 C-G	46 A-D	47 B-F	48 C-H	49 E-G

16 ENTRIES

Two Playing Areas

See Round Robin Eight Entries—One Playing Area

Three Playing Areas

POOL 1		POOL 2	
PA I	PA II	PA II	PA III
1 F-H			2 F-H
3 B-C	4 D-G		5 B-C
6 A-E		7 D-G	8 A-E
9 B-H	10 C-F		11 B-H
12 D-E		13 C-F	14 D-E
15 A-G	16 D-H		17 A-G
18 A-C		19 A-C	20 D-H
21 B-E	22 F-G		23 B-E
24 A-H		25 F-G	26 A-H
27 B-G	28 E-F		29 B-G
30 C-D		31 E-F	32 C-D
33 A-B	34 D-F		35 A-B
36 C-E		37 D-F	38 C-E
39 G-H	40 B-D		41 G-H
42 A-F		43 B-D	44 A-F
45 E-H	46 A-D		47 E-H
48 C-G		49 A-D	50 C-G
51 B-F	52 C-H		53 B-F
54 E-G		55 C-H	56 E-G

Four Playing Areas

POOL 1		POOL 2	
PA I	PA II	PA III	PA IV
1 A-B	2 C-D	3 A-B	4 C-D
5 E-F	6 G-H	7 E-F	8 G-H
9 B-E	10 A-C	11 B-E	12 A-C
13 D-G	14 F-H	15 D-G	16 F-H
17 C-G	18 A-E	19 C-G	20 A-E
21 B-H	22 D-F	23 B-H	24 D-F
25 E-H	26 A-G	27 E-H	28 A-G
29 C-F	30 B-D	31 C-F	32 B-D
33 A-H	34 F-G	35 A-H	36 F-G
37 D-E	38 B-C	39 D-E	40 B-C
41 A-F	42 D-H	43 A-F	44 D-H
45 B-G	46 C-E	47 B-G	48 C-E
49 A-D	50 B-F	51 A-D	52 B-F
53 C-H	54 E-G	55 C-H	56 E-G

FOR ROUND ROBIN—DOUBLE SPLIT TOURNAMENTS

Five Playing Areas

	POOL 1			POOL 2	
PA I	PA II	PA III	PA III	PA IV	PA V
1 A-B					
2 C-D	3 E-F		4 E-F	5 C-D	6 A-B
7 G-H	8 B-E	9 A-C		10 B-E	11 G-H
12 F-H	13 D-G		14 A-C	15 D-G	16 F-H
17 A-E	18 C-G	19 B-H		20 C-G	21 A-E
22 E-H	23 D-F		24 B-H	25 A-G	26 D-F
27 C-F	28 B-D	29 A-G		30 E-H	31 C-F
32 F-G	33 A-H		34 B-D	35 A-H	36 F-G
37 B-C	38 A-F	39 D-E		40 B-C	41 D-E
42 D-H	43 B-G		44 D-H	45 A-F	46 B-G
47 A-D	48 C-E	49 B-F		50 C-E	51 A-D
52 E-G	53 C-H		54 E-G	55 B-F	56 C-H

Six Playing Areas

	POOL 1			POOL 2	
PA I	PA II	PA III	PA IV	PA V	PA VI
1 A-B			2 A-B		
3 C-D	4 G-H	5 E-F	6 C-D	7 G-H	8 E-F
9 F-G	10 A-H	11 D-E	12 F-G	13 A-H	14 D-E
15 B-C	16 A-F	17 D-H	18 B-C	19 A-F	20 D-H
21 A-C	22 B-E	23 D-G	24 A-C	25 B-E	26 D-G
27 F-H	28 C-G	29 A-E	30 F-H	31 C-G	32 A-E
33 E-H	34 B-D	35 C-F	36 E-H	37 B-D	38 C-F
39 B-H	40 D-F	41 A-G	42 B-H	43 D-F	44 A-G
45 A-D	46 C-E	47 B-G	48 A-D	49 C-E	50 B-G
51 E-G	52 B-F	53 C-H	54 E-G	55 B-F	56 C-H

Seven Playing Areas

	POOL 1				POOL 2		
PA I	PA II	PA III	PA IV	PA V	PA VI	PA VII	PA VIII
1 E-F	2 C-D	3 A-B	4 G-H		5 E-F	6 C-D	7 A-B
8 D-G	9 F-H	10 B-E	11 A-C		12 G-H	13 B-E	14 A-C
15 C-G	16 A-E	17 B-H	18 D-F		19 D-G	20 C-G	21 F-H
22 E-H	23 A-G	24 C-F	25 B-D		26 A-E	27 B-H	28 D-F
29 A-H	30 D-E	31 F-G		32 E-H	33 C-F	34 A-G	35 B-D
36 A-F	37 B-C	38 D-H		39 F-G	40 B-C	41 D-E	42 A-H
43 B-G	44 C-E	45 A-D		46 B-G	47 D-H	48 A-F	49 C-E
50 C-H	51 B-F	52 E-G		53 A-D	54 B-F	55 C-H	56 E-G

(continued)

PLAYING SCHEDULES

FOR ROUND ROBIN—DOUBLE SPLIT TOURNAMENTS

Eight Playing Areas

	POOL 1				POOL 2		
PA I	PA II	PA III	PA IV	PA V	PA VI	PA VII	PA VIII
1 G-H	2 A-B	3 E-F	4 C-D	5 G-H	6 A-B	7 E-F	8 C-D
9 F-H	10 D-G	11 A-C	12 B-E	13 F-H	14 D-G	15 A-C	16 B-E
17 C-G	18 A-E	19 B-H	20 D-F	21 C-G	22 A-E	23 B-H	24 D-F
25 B-D	26 C-F	27 A-G	28 E-H	29 B-D	30 C-F	31 A-G	32 E-H
33 B-C	34 F-G	35 D-E	36 A-H	37 B-C	38 F-G	39 D-E	40 A-H
41 E-C	42 D-H	43 B-G	44 A-F	45 E-C	46 D-H	47 B-G	48 A-F
49 A-D	50 B-F	51 C-H	52 E-G	53 A-D	54 B-F	55 C-H	56 E-G

PLAYING SCHEDULES
FOR ROUND ROBIN—TRIPLE SPLIT TOURNAMENTS

NINE ENTRIES

Two Playing Areas

POOL 1	POOL 2		POOL 3	
PA II	PA II	PA I	PA I	
		1 A-B		
2 A-B			3 A-B	
4 B-C		5 B-C		
6 A-C			7 B-C	
	8 A-C		9 A-C	

Three Playing Areas

POOL 1	POOL 2	POOL 3
PA I	PA II	PA III
1 A-B	2 A-B	3 A-B
4 B-C	5 B-C	6 B-C
7 A-C	8 A-C	9 A-C

10 ENTRIES

Two Playing Areas

POOL 1	POOL 2	POOL 3
PA I	PA I	PA II
1 A-B		2 A-C
	3 A-B	4 B-D
5 B-C		6 A-D
	7 B-C	8 B-C
9 A-C		10 A-B
	11 A-C	12 C-D

Three Playing Areas

POOL 1	POOL 2		POOL 3	
PA I	PA I	PA II	PA II	PA III
1 A-B			2 A-C	3 B-D
4 B-C		5 A-B		6 A-D
7 A-C		8 B-C		9 B-C
	10 A-C		11 C-D	12 A-B

Four Playing Areas

POOL 1	POOL 2	POOL 3	
PA I	PA II	PA III	PA IV
1 A-B	2 A-B	3 A-C	4 B-D
5 B-C	6 B-C	7 A-D	8 B-C
9 A-C	10 A-C	11 C-D	12 A-B

(continued)

PLAYING SCHEDULES
FOR ROUND ROBIN—TRIPLE SPLIT TOURNAMENTS

11 ENTRIES

Two Playing Areas

POOL 1		POOL 2		POOL 3	
PA I		PA I	PA II	PA II	
		1 A-C			
		2 B-D		3 A-C	
		4 A-D		5 B-D	
6 A-B				7 A-D	
		8 B-C		9 B-C	
10 B-C			11 A-B		
		12 C-D		13 A-B	
14 A-C				15 C-D	

Three Playing Areas

POOL 1		POOL 2		POOL 3	
PA I	PA I	PA II	PA III	PA II	PA III
	1 A-C			2 A-C	3 B-D
	4 B-D			5 A-D	6 B-C
7 A-B		8 A-D	9 B-C		
10 B-C		11 A-B			12 A-B
13 A-C		14 C-D			15 C-D

Four Playing Areas

POOL 1		POOL 2		POOL 3
PA I	PA II	PA II	PA III	PA IV
1 A-C	2 B-D		3 A-C	4 A-B
5 B-C	6 A-D		7 B-D	8 B-C
9 A-B		10 A-D	11 B-C	12 A-C
13 C-D		14 C-D	15 A-B	

Five Playing Areas

POOL 1	POOL 2		POOL 3	
PA I	PA II	PA III	PA IV	PA V
1 A-B	2 A-C	3 B-D	4 A-C	5 B-D
6 B-C	7 A-D	8 B-C	9 A-D	10 B-C
11 A-C	12 A-B	13 C-D	14 A-B	15 C-D

PLAYING SCHEDULES

FOR ROUND ROBIN—TRIPLE SPLIT TOURNAMENTS

12 ENTRIES

Two Playing Areas

POOL 1			POOL 2			POOL 3
PA I		PA I	PA II			PA II
1 A-C						2 A-C
3 B-D			4 A-C			
		5 B-D				6 B-D
7 A-D						8 A-D
9 B-C			10 A-D			
		11 B-C				12 B-C
13 A-B			14 A-B			
15 C-D						16 A-B
		17 C-D				18 C-D

Three Playing Areas

POOL 1	POOL 2	POOL 3
PA I	PA II	PA III
1 A-C	2 A-C	3 A-C
4 B-D	5 B-D	6 B-D
7 A-D	8 A-D	9 A-D
10 B-C	11 B-C	12 B-C
13 A-B	14 A-B	15 A-B
16 C-D	17 C-D	18 C-D

Four Playing Areas

POOL 1		POOL 2		POOL 3	
PA I	PA II	PA II	PA III	PA III	PA IV
1 A-C	2 B-D				
3 A-D		4 A-C	5 B-D		6 A-C
7 B-C		8 A-D	9 B-C		10 B-D
11 A-B		12 A-B		13 A-D	14 B-C
15 C-D		16 C-D		17 C-D	18 A-B

Five Playing Areas

POOL 1		POOL 2			POOL 3	
PA I	PA II	PA II	PA III	PA IV	PA IV	PA V
1 A-C	2 B-D					3 A-C
4 A-D	5 B-C		6 A-C	7 B-D		8 B-D
9 A-B		10 A-D	11 B-C		12 A-D	13 B-C
14 C-D		15 C-D	16 A-B		17 C-D	18 A-B

Six Playing Areas

POOL 1		POOL 2		POOL 3	
PA I	PA II	PA III	PA IV	PA V	PA VI
1 A-C	2 B-D	3 A-C	4 B-D	5 A-C	6 B-D
7 A-D	8 B-C	9 A-D	10 B-C	11 A-D	12 B-C
13 C-D	14 A-B	15 C-D	16 A-B	17 C-D	18 A-B

(continued)

PLAYING SCHEDULES

FOR ROUND ROBIN—TRIPLE SPLIT TOURNAMENTS

13 ENTRIES

Two Playing Areas

POOL 1	POOL 2		POOL 3
PA I	PA I	PA II	PA II
1 A-C		2 A-C	
3 B-D			4 A-B
	5 B-D		6 C-D
7 A-D			8 B-E
	9 A-D		10 A-C
11 B-C			12 D-E
	13 B-C		14 B-C
15 A-B			16 A-D
	17 A-B		18 C-E
19 C-D			20 B-D
	21 C-D		22 A-E

Three Playing Areas

POOL 1	POOL 2		POOL 3
PA I	PA II	PA II	PA III
1 A-B	2 C-D		
3 B-E	4 A-C	5 A-C	6 A-C
	7 D-E	8 B-D	9 B-D
	10 B-C	11 A-D	12 A-D
	13 A-D	14 B-C	15 B-C
	16 C-E	17 A-B	18 A-B
	19 B-D	20 C-D	21 C-D
	22 A-E		

Four Playing Areas

POOL 1	POOL 2	POOL 3	
PA I	PA II	PA III	PA IV
1 A-C	2 A-C		
3 B-D	4 B-D	5 A-D	6 B-C
7 A-D	8 A-D	9 A-C	10 D-E
11 B-C	12 B-C	13 B-E	14 C-D
15 A-B	16 A-B	17 C-E	18 A-B
19 C-D	20 C-D	21 B-D	22 A-E

Five Playing Areas

POOL 1		POOL 2		POOL 3	
PA I	PA II	PA III	PA IV	PA IV	PA V
1 C-E	2 A-D				
3 A-C	4 B-E	5 A-C	6 B-D		7 A-C
8 A-B	9 C-D	10 A-D	11 B-C		12 B-D
13 D-E	14 B-C	15 A-B		16 A-D	17 B-C
18 B-D	19 A-E	20 C-D		21 C-D	22 A-B

Six Playing Areas

POOL 1		POOL 2		POOL 3	
PA I	PA II	PA III	PA IV	PA V	PA VI
1 C-E	2 A-D				
3 A-C	4 B-E				
5 A-B	6 C-D	7 A-C	8 B-D	9 A-C	10 B-D
11 D-E	12 B-C	13 A-D	14 B-C	15 A-D	16 B-C
17 B-D	18 A-E	19 C-D	20 A-B	21 C-D	22 A-B

PLAYING SCHEDULES

FOR ROUND ROBIN—TRIPLE SPLIT TOURNAMENTS

14 ENTRIES

Two Playing Areas

POOL 1	POOL 2		POOL 3
PA I	PA I	PA II	PA II
	1 A-B		2 A-B
3 A-C			4 C-D
5 B-D		6 C-D	
	7 B-E		8 B-E
	9 A-C		10 A-C
11 A-D		12 D-E	
13 B-C		14 B-C	
	15 A-D		16 D-E
	17 C-E		18 B-C
19 A-B			20 A-D
21 C-D			22 C-E
	23 B-D		24 B-D
	25 A-E		26 A-E

Three Playing Areas

POOL 1	POOL 2		POOL 3	
PA I	PA I	PA II	PA II	PA III
	1 A-B	2 C-D		
3 A-C		4 B-E		5 A-B
6 B-D		7 A-C		8 C-D
	9 D-E		10 B-E	11 A-C
	12 B-C		13 D-E	14 B-C
15 A-D		16 A-D		17 A-D
18 B-C		19 C-E		20 C-E
21 A-B		22 B-D		23 B-D
24 C-D		25 A-E		26 A-E

Four Playing Areas

POOL 1		POOL 2		POOL 3
PA I	PA II	PA II	PA III	PA IV
1 A-B	2 C-D			
3 B-E		4 C-E	5 A-D	6 A-C
7 A-C		8 A-B	9 C-D	10 B-D
11 D-E	12 B-C		13 B-E	14 A-D
15 A-D	16 C-E		17 A-C	18 B-C
19 B-D		20 D-E	21 B-C	22 A-B
23 A-E		24 B-D	25 A-E	26 C-D

(continued)

FOR ROUND ROBIN—TRIPLE SPLIT TOURNAMENTS

Five Playing Areas

POOL 1		POOL 2		POOL 3	
PA I	PA II	PA III	PA IV	PA V	
1 A-C					
2 B-D	3 C-E	4 A-D	5 C-E	6 A-D	
7 A-D	8 A-C	9 B-E	10 A-C	11 B-E	
12 B-C	13 A-B	14 C-D	15 A-B	16 C-D	
17 A-B	18 D-E	19 B-C	20 D-E	21 B-C	
22 C-D	23 B-D	24 A-E	25 B-D	26 A-E	

Six Playing Areas

POOL 1		POOL 2		POOL 3	
PA I	PA II	PA III	PA IV	PA V	PA VI
1 C-E	2 A-D	3 C-E	4 A-D		
5 A-C	6 B-E	7 A-C	8 B-E		
9 A-B	10 C-D	11 A-B	12 C-D	13 A-C	14 B-D
15 D-E	16 B-C	17 D-E	18 B-C	19 A-D	20 B-C
21 B-D	22 A-E	23 B-D	24 A-E	25 C-D	26 A-B

15 ENTRIES

Three Playing Areas

POOL 1	POOL 2	POOL 3
PA I	PA II	PA III
1 A-B	2 A-B	3 A-B
4 C-D	5 C-D	6 C-D
7 B-E	8 B-E	9 B-E
10 A-C	11 A-C	12 A-C
13 D-E	14 D-E	15 D-E
16 B-C	17 B-C	18 B-C
19 A-D	20 A-D	21 A-D
22 C-E	23 C-E	24 C-E
25 B-D	26 B-D	27 B-D
28 A-E	29 A-E	30 A-E

Four Playing Areas

POOL 1		POOL 2		POOL 3	
PA I	PA II	PA II	PA III	PA III	PA IV
1 A-B			2 A-B		3 C-E
4 C-D			5 C-D		6 A-D
7 B-E	8 A-C		9 B-E		10 A-C
11 D-E	12 B-C		13 A-C		14 B-E
15 A-D		16 D-E	17 B-C		18 C-D
19 C-E		20 A-D	21 C-E		22 A-B
23 B-D		24 B-D		25 D-E	26 B-C
27 A-E		28 A-E		29 A-E	30 B-D

PLAYING SCHEDULES

FOR ROUND ROBIN—TRIPLE SPLIT TOURNAMENTS

Five Playing Areas

| POOL 1 | | POOL 2 | | POOL 3 | | |
PA I	PA II	PA II	PA III	PA IV	PA IV	PA V
1 A-B	2 C-D		3 C-E	4 A-D		5 C-E
6 B-E	7 A-C		8 A-C	9 B-E		10 A-D
11 D-E	12 B-C		13 C-D		14 A-C	15 B-E
16 A-D	17 C-E		18 A-B		19 A-B	20 C-D
21 B-D		22 D-E	23 B-C		24 D-E	25 B-C
26 A-E		27 A-E	28 B-D		29 B-D	30 A-E

Six Playing Areas

| POOL 1 | | POOL 2 | | POOL 3 | |
PA I	PA II	PA III	PA IV	PA V	PA VI
1 C-E	2 A-D	3 C-E	4 A-D	5 C-E	6 A-D
7 A-C	8 B-E	9 A-C	10 B-E	11 A-C	12 B-E
13 A-B	14 C-D	15 A-B	16 C-D	17 A-B	18 C-D
19 D-E	20 B-C	21 D-E	22 B-C	23 D-E	24 B-C
25 B-D	26 A-E	27 B-D	28 A-E	29 B-D	30 A-E

16 ENTRIES

Three Playing Areas

| POOL 1 | | | POOL 2 | POOL 3 |
PA I	PA II	PA III	PA II	PA III
1 C-D	2 A-B			
3 A-C	4 E-F			5 A-B
6 B-E		7 F-D	8 A-B	
9 A-E			10 C-D	11 C-D
12 C-F			13 B-E	14 B-E
15 B-D			16 A-C	17 A-C
18 A-F			19 D-E	20 D-E
21 D-E			22 B-C	23 B-C
24 B-C			25 A-D	26 A-D
27 A-D			28 C-E	29 C-E
30 B-F			31 B-D	32 B-D
33 C-E			34 A-E	35 A-E

(continued)

PLAYING SCHEDULES

FOR ROUND ROBIN—TRIPLE SPLIT TOURNAMENTS

Four Playing Areas

POOL 1 PA I	POOL 1 PA II	POOL 1 PA III	POOL 2 PA II	POOL 2 PA III	POOL 3 PA III	POOL 3 PA IV
3 E-F	2 C-D	1 A-B				
7 A-C	6 B-E	5 D-F				
11 A-E						4 A-B
15 C-F			10 C-D	9 A-B		8 C-D
19 B-D			14 B-E		13 A-C	12 B-E
23 A-F			18 A-C		17 B-C	16 D-E
27 D-E			22 B-C	21 D-E		20 A-D
31 A-D	30 B-C		26 C-E	25 A-D		24 C-E
35 C-E	34 B-F			29 B-D		28 B-D
				33 A-E		32 A-E

Five Playing Areas

POOL 1 PA I	POOL 1 PA II	POOL 2 PA II	POOL 2 PA III	POOL 3 PA III	POOL 3 PA IV	POOL 3 PA V
1 A-B	2 C-D			3 A-B	4 C-D	5 E-F
6 B-E		7 C-E	8 A-D		9 A-C	10 B-E
11 A-C		12 A-B	13 C-D		14 D-F	15 A-E
16 D-E	17 B-C		18 B-E		19 C-F	20 B-D
21 A-D	22 C-E		23 A-C		24 D-E	25 A-F
26 B-D		27 D-E	28 B-C		29 B-C	30 A-D
31 A-E		32 B-D	33 A-E		34 B-F	35 C-E

Six Playing Areas

POOL 1 PA I	POOL 1 PA II	POOL 2 PA II	POOL 2 PA III	POOL 2 PA IV	POOL 3 PA IV	POOL 3 PA V	POOL 3 PA VI
1 C-E	2 A-D				3 A-B	4 E-F	5 C-D
6 A-C		7 C-E	8 A-D		9 D-F	10 A-C	11 B-E
12 B-E		13 A-C	14 B-E		15 A-E	16 B-D	17 C-F
18 A-B	19 C-D		20 C-D	21 A-B		22 A-F	23 D-E
24 D-E	25 B-C		26 B-C	27 D-E		28 B-C	29 A-D
30 B-D	31 A-E		32 A-E	33 B-D		34 C-E	35 B-F

Seven Playing Areas

POOL 1 PA I	POOL 1 PA II	POOL 2 PA III	POOL 2 PA IV	POOL 2 PA V	POOL 3 PA VI	POOL 3 PA VII
1 C-E	2 A-D	3 C-E	4 A-D	5 A-B	6 E-F	7 C-D
8 A-C	9 B-E	10 A-C	11 B-E	12 D-F	13 A-C	14 B-E
15 A-B	16 C-D	17 A-B	18 C-D	19 A-E	20 B-D	21 C-F
22 D-E	23 B-C	24 D-E	25 B-C	26 B-C	27 D-E	28 A-F
29 B-D	30 A-E	31 B-D	32 A-E	33 C-E	34 B-F	35 A-D

PLAYING SCHEDULES

FOR ROUND ROBIN—QUADRUPLE SPLIT TOURNAMENTS

12 ENTRIES

Two Playing Areas

POOL 1	POOL 2	POOL 3	POOL 4
PA I	PA I	PA II	PA II
1 A-B		2 A-B	
	3 A-B		4 A-B
5 B-C		6 B-C	
	7 B-C		8 B-C
9 A-C		10 A-C	
	11 A-C		12 A-C

Three Playing Areas

POOL 1		POOL 2		POOL 3		POOL 4
PA I	PA I	PA II	PA II	PA III	PA III	
1 A-B		2 A-B		3 A-B		
4 B-C		5 B-C			6 A-B	
7 A-C			8 B-C		9 B-C	
	10 A-C		11 A-C		12 A-C	

Four Playing Areas

POOL 1	POOL 2	POOL 3	POOL 4
PA I	PA II	PA III	PA IV
1 A-B	2 A-B	3 A-B	4 A-B
5 B-C	6 B-C	7 B-C	8 B-C
9 A-C	10 A-C	11 A-C	12 A-C

13 ENTRIES

Two Playing Areas

POOL 1	POOL 2		POOL 3	POOL 4
PA I	PA I	PA II	PA II	PA II
1 A-C				
2 B-D		3 A-B		
4 A-D			5 A-B	
	6 B-C			7 A-B
8 B-C			9 B-C	
	10 A-C			11 B-C
12 A-B			13 A-C	
14 C-D				15 A-C

(continued)

PLAYING SCHEDULES

FOR ROUND ROBIN—QUADRUPLE SPLIT TOURNAMENTS

Three Playing Areas

POOL 1	POOL 2		POOL 3		POOL 4	
PA I	PA I	PA II	PA II	PA III	PA II	PA III
1 A-B					2 A-C	3 B-D
	4 A-B		5 A-B			6 A-D
7 B-C			8 B-C			9 B-C
	10 B-C				11 A-B	12 C-D
13 A-C		14 A-C		15 A-C		

Four Playing Areas

POOL 1	POOL 2	POOL 3	POOL 4			
PA I	PA II	PA III	PA I	PA II	PA III	PA IIV
1 A-B	2 A-B	3 A-B				
4 B-C	5 B-C				6 A-C	7 B-D
8 A-C		9 B-C		10 A-D		11 B-C
	12 A-C	13 A-C	14 A-B			15 C-D

Five Playing Areas

POOL 1	POOL 2	POOL 3	POOL 4	
PA I	PA II	PA III	PA IV	PA V
1 A-B	2 A-B	3 A-B	4 A-D	5 B-C
6 B-C	7 B-C	8 B-C	9 B-D	10 A-C
11 A-C	12 A-C	13 A-C	14 A-B	15 C-D

14 ENTRIES

Two Playing Areas

POOL 1	POOL 2		POOL 3	POOL 4
PA I	PA I	PA II	PA II	PA II
1 A-D		2 A-D		
3 B-C			4 A-B	
	5 B-C			6 A-B
7 B-D		8 B-D		
	9 A-C		10 B-C	
11 A-C				12 B-C
13 A-B		14 A-B		
	15 C-D		16 A-C	
17 C-D				18 A-C

PLAYING SCHEDULES
FOR ROUND ROBIN—QUADRUPLE SPLIT TOURNAMENTS

Three Playing Areas

POOL 3	POOL 2	POOL 3	POOL 4
PA I	PA I	PA II	PA III
1 A-B		2 A-D	3 A-D
	4 A-B	5 B-C	6 B-C
7 B-C		8 B-D	9 B-D
	10 B-C	11 A-C	12 A-C
13 A-C		14 A-B	15 A-B
	16 A-C	17 C-D	18 C-D

Four Playing Areas

POOL 1	POOL 2		POOL 3			POOL 4	
PA I	PA II	PA I	PA II	PA III		PA III	PA IV
		1 A-D	2 B-C			3 B-C	4 A-D
5 A-B	6 A-B						
		7 B-D	8 A-C			9 B-D	10 A-C
11 B-C	12 B-C			13 A-B			14 A-B
15 A-C	16 A-C			17 C-D			18 C-D

Five Playing Areas

POOL 1		POOL 2		POOL 3	POOL 4
PA I	PA II	PA II	PA III	PA IV	PA V
1 A-D	2 B-C		3 A-D		
4 B-D	5 A-C		6 B-C	7 A-B	8 A-B
9 A-B		10 B-D	11 A-C	12 B-C	13 B-C
14 C-D		15 A-B	16 C-D	17 A-C	18 A-C

Six Playing Areas

POOL 1	POOL 2	POOL 3		POOL 4	
PA I	PA II	PA III	PA IV	PA V	PA VI
1 A-B	2 A-B	3 A-D	4 B-C	5 A-D	6 B-C
7 B-C	8 B-C	9 B-D	10 A-C	11 B-D	12 A-C
13 A-C	14 A-C	15 A-B	16 C-D	17 A-B	18 C-D

(continued)

PLAYING SCHEDULES

FOR ROUND ROBIN–QUADRUPLE SPLIT TOURNAMENTS

Two Playing Areas

POOL 1 PA I	POOL 2 PA I	POOL 3 PA I	POOL 3 PA II	POOL 4 PA II
	1 A-D			
		2 A-D		
				3 A-D
	4 B-C			
				5 B-C
	6 B-D			
			7 B-C	
8 A-B				
				9 B-D
		10 B-D		
				11 A-C
	12 A-C			
			13 A-C	
14 B-C				
				15 A-B
	16 A-B			
			17 A-B	
	18 C-D			
				19 C-D
20 A-C				
			21 A-D	

Three Playing Areas

POOL 1 PA I	POOL 1 PA II	POOL 1 PA III	POOL 2 PA I	POOL 3 PA II	POOL 4 PA III
			1 A-D	2 A-D	3 A-D
			4 B-C	5 B-C	6 B-C
		7 A-B	8 B-D	9 B-D	
			10 A-C	11 A-C	12 B-D
	13 B-C		14 A-B		15 A-C
			16 C-D	17 A-B	18 A-B
19 A-C				20 C-D	21 C-D

Four Playing Areas

POOL 1 PA II	POOL 2 PA II	POOL 2 PA I	POOL 3 PA I	POOL 3 PA III	POOL 3 PA IV	POOL 4 PA III	POOL 4 PA IV
		1 A-C					
2 A-B		3 B-D		4 A-C			5 A-C
	6 A-D	7 B-C		8 B-D			9 B-D
10 B-C		11 A-B		12 A-D	13 B-C		
	14 C-D		15 A-B			16 A-D	17 B-C
18 A-C			19 C-D			20 A-B	21 C-D

Five Playing Areas

POOL 1 PA II	POOL 2 PA II	POOL 2 PA I	POOL 3 PA III	POOL 3 PA IV	POOL 4 PA IV	POOL 4 PA V
		1 A-C				
2 A-B		3 B-D	4 A-C	5 B-D		6 A-C
	7 A-D	8 B-C	9 A-D	10 B-C		11 B-D
12 B-C		13 A-B	14 A-B		15 A-D	16 B-C
17 A-C		18 C-D	19 C-D		20 A-B	21 C-D

FOR ROUND ROBIN—QUADRUPLE SPLIT TOURNAMENTS

Six Playing Areas

POOL 1	POOL 2		POOL 3		POOL 4	
PA I	PA II	PA III	PA III	PA IV	PA V	PA VI
	1 A-C	2 B-D		3 A-C		
4 A-B	5 A-D	6 B-C		7 B-D	8 A-C	9 B-D
10 B-C	11 A-B		12 A-D	13 B-C	14 A-D	15 B-C
16 A-C	17 C-D		18 A-B	19 C-D	20 A-B	21 C-D

Seven Playing Areas

POOL 1	POOL 2		POOL 3		POOL 4	
PA I	PA II	PA III	PA IV	PA V	PA VI	PA VII
1 A-B	2 A-C	3 B-D	4 A-C	5 B-D	6 A-C	7 B-D
8 B-C	9 A-D	10 B-C	11 A-D	12 B-C	13 A-D	14 B-C
15 A-C	16 A-B	17 C-D	18 A-B	19 C-D	20 A-B	21 C-D

Two Playing Areas

POOL 1	POOL 2	POOL 3	POOL 4
PA I	PA I	PA II	PA II
1 A-C		2 A-C	
	3 A-C		4 A-C
5 B-D		6 B-D	
	7 B-D		8 B-D
9 A-D		10 A-D	
	11 A-D		12 A-D
13 B-C		14 B-C	
	15 B-C		16 B-C
17 A-B		18 A-B	
	19 A-B		20 A-B
21 C-D		22 C-D	
	23 C-D		24 C-D

Three Playing Areas

POOL 1	POOL 2		POOL 3		POOL 4
PA I	PA I	PA II	PA II	PA III	PA III
1 A-C		2 A-C		3 A-C	
4 B-D		5 B-D			6 A-C
7 A-D			8 B-D		9 B-D
	10 A-D		11 A-D		12 A-D
13 B-C		14 B-C		15 B-C	
16 A-B		17 A-B			18 B-C
19 C-D			20 A-B		21 A-B
	22 C-D		23 C-D		24 C-D

(continued)

PLAYING SCHEDULES

FOR ROUND ROBIN—QUADRUPLE SPLIT TOURNAMENTS

Four Playing Areas

POOL 1	POOL 2	POOL 3	POOL 4
PA I	PA II	PA III	PA IV
1 A-C	2 A-C	3 A-C	4 A-C
5 B-D	6 B-D	7 B-D	8 B-D
9 A-D	10 A-D	11 A-D	12 A-D
13 B-C	14 B-C	15 B-C	16 B-C
17 A-B	18 A-B	19 A-B	20 A-B
21 C-D	22 C-D	23 C-D	24 C-D

Five Playing Areas

POOL 1		POOL 2		POOL 3			POOL 4	
PA I	PA II	PA II	PA III	PA III	PA IV	PA V	PA IV	PA V
1 A-C	2 B-D		3 A-C		4 A-C			5 A-C
6 A-D			7 B-D		8 B-D			9 B-D
10 B-C		11 A-D	12 B-C		13 A-D	14 B-C		
15 A-B		16 A-B		17 A-B			18 A-D	19 B-C
20 C-D		21 C-D		22 C-D			23 A-B	24 C-D

Six Playing Areas

POOL 1		POOL 2		POOL 3		POOL 4	
PA I	PA II	PA II	PA III	PA IV	PA V	PA V	PA VI
1 A-C	2 B-D		3 A-C	4 A-C	5 B-D		6 A-C
7 A-D	8 B-C		9 B-D	10 A-D	11 B-C		12 B-D
13 A-B		14 A-D	15 B-C	16 A-B		17 A-D	18 B-C
19 C-D		20 A-B	21 C-D	22 C-D		23 A-B	24 C-D

Seven Playing Areas

POOL 1		POOL 2		POOL 3		POOL 4	
PA I	PA II	PA II	PA III	PA IV	PA V	PA VI	PA VII
1 A-C	2 B-D		3 A-C				
4 A-D	5 B-C		6 B-D	7 A-C	8 B-D	9 A-C	10 B-D
11 A-B		12 A-D	13 B-C	14 A-D	15 B-C	16 A-D	17 B-C
18 C-D		19 A-B	20 C-D	21 A-B	22 C-D	23 A-B	24 C-D

Eight Playing Areas

POOL 1		POOL 2		POOL 3		POOL 4	
PA I	PA II	PA III	PA IV	PA V	PA VI	PA VII	PA VIII
1 A-C	2 B-D	3 A-C	4 B-D	5 A-C	6 B-D	7 A-C	8 B-D
9 A-D	10 B-C	11 A-D	12 B-C	13 A-D	14 B-C	15 A-D	16 B-C
17 A-B	18 C-D	19 A-B	20 C-D	21 A-B	22 C-D	23 A-B	24 C-D

CHAPTER 6

Extended Tournaments

Advantages	Disadvantages
• You can conduct them over any length of time.	• The number of games depends on the entrant's initiative in challenging.
• The number of games per entry *can* be unlimited.	
• They require little supervision.	
• No one is eliminated.	

Best use: Individual sports in recreational settings

■ An extended tournament, as the name implies, can go on indefinitely. This type of tournament is often used for dual activities, particularly racquet sports. As an ongoing tournament in intramurals or even in a physical education class, this type of tournament can be effective. Entries challenge players above them, and therefore the schedule of games is up to the players themselves.

Though you can produce large, extended tournaments, it is usually more effective to limit the size, perhaps to 15. If you had more than 15 entries, you might wish to create two or three extended tournaments, each reflecting a different level of play—perhaps with the categories of novice, intermediate, and advanced.

It is possible for this type of tournament to go on forever, but that is usually not desirable. You may want to set a time limit on the tournament or to announce at fixed times who is leading. The most popular versions of this type of tournament are the ladder and the pyramid. There are also other types that work effectively. Because these tournaments are ongoing, the participants often change their positions on the tournament board by themselves. If the extended tournament is being held in a YMCA or racquet club, it may be helpful to include a phone number for each entry so players can arrange their contests.

In the case of racquet clubs or intramurals, you may find that not all entries are participating, even though they signed up for the tournament. To ensure that all participants are active, you might ask players to write the date of their last game on the back of their identifying marker, and remove entries that have not played for a specified time. A period of one week is usually sufficient. In a physical education class or other setting in which you want all entries to be actively participating, you might add rules to ensure that this happens. For example, suppose two entries continually challenge each other and play no one else; a rule stating that an entry cannot play the same opponent twice in a row would help solve this problem.

To ensure evenly matched games and a tournament that reflects the different calibers of play, players should play only those one or two levels removed from their level. The most common rule is that a player can play someone at a lower level only when they are challenged by such an entry. A second common rule is that you can challenge someone one or two levels up from yourself, but no further. In the extended tournaments, if the challenger wins, the challenger exchanges places with the entry challenged.

There are several common ways to assign initial positions to entries at the start of an extended tournament. The easiest is to assign them randomly. This encourages players to challenge each other as they rise and fall to their levels of play. Another way is to seed the entries and place them in reverse order onto the tournament. With the weakest players on the top and the strongest on the bottom, the strongest are encouraged to challenge the other entries to achieve as high a spot on the tournament as possible. A third approach is to seed and place entries where you feel they should be. This decreases the number of lopsided games but provides less incentive for players to challenge each other.

Ladder Tournament

This is probably the most common extended tournament. As the name implies, this tournament format looks like a ladder, with an entry on each rung. The objective is to work your way up the ladder by winning games against those higher than you.

There are many ways to construct a layout for this tournament; we list some at the end of this chapter. One suggestion is to use tongue depressors as rungs on which you print names, as shown in figure 6.1. Make holes in each end of the rungs, which fit over hooks fastened to the uprights. Print numbers with the contestants' starting positions to show advancement.

Pyramid Tournament

This type of tournament is similar to the ladder tournament except that many participants may be on the same level. As in the ladder tournament, entries can only challenge one or two levels up from their positions. The advantage is that instead of a single player at the bottom, as in the ladder tournament, several players share that position. Figure 6.2 illustrates what such a tournament would

Figure 6.1 Ladder tournament.

look like. A useful variation on the pyramid tournament is the crown tournament, sometimes referred to as the king tournament (see figure 6.3). This tournament is made up of several pyramids, each having 10 spaces, at different levels. Challenging is vertical within each pyramid and horizontal among pyramids. The object is to advance as high up the pyramids as possible. You may add more pyramids to the pattern if there are enough participants.

Another variation on the pyramid tournament is a spiderweb tournament, shown in figure 6.4. The object of this tournament is to work your way as close to the center as possible. The advantage of the spiderweb is that it can accommodate more contestants in its diagram. The disadvantage, however, is that as the center or winner's position is approached, the number of contestants remains the same as in the outer ring. In figure 6.4, eight contestants are vying for the center position. This tournament forces the player in the center to play numerous matches.

Level Rotation

This type is much like the ladder tournament except that the challenges are built in and you need keep no record about who is playing whom. This ensures that all participants play and none are left out. This tournament type is especially helpful if the activity requires changing positions many times, as in a series of combatives

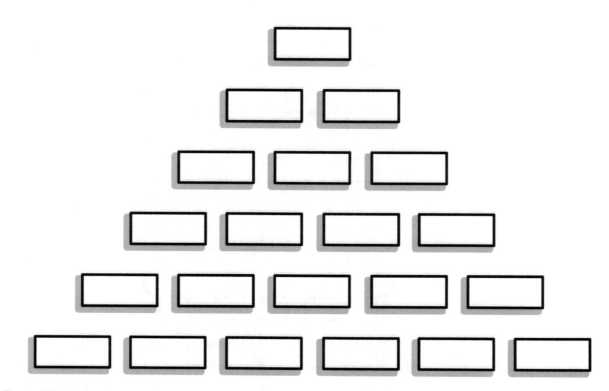

Figure 6.2 Pyramid tournament.

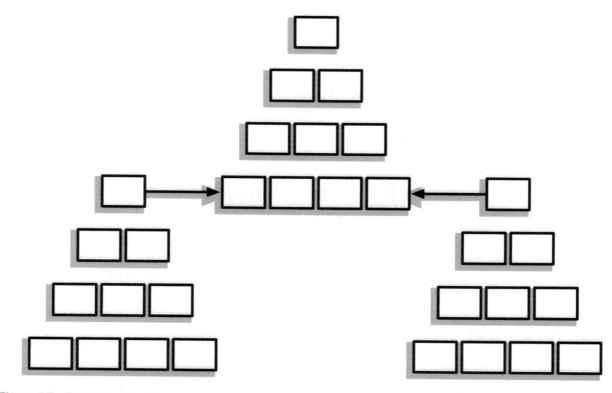

Figure 6.3 Crown tournament.

Figure 6.4 Spider web tournament.

or short badminton games. For example, a teacher may wish to have students play a series of five-minute badminton games, rotating after each game. In this case, a level-rotation tournament structure will prove effective and easy to use, especially because you write nothing down.

The instructions are simple: When the activity is completed, the winners move one playing area over in one direction, and the losers move one playing area over in the other direction. The net result is that participants of similar ability play each other.

To illustrate this, we show an example in figure 6.5. The numbers refer to the players' level. The illustration has players assigned randomly in the first game. After the first game, seed number 10 has lost and therefore moves to the right, as

<table>
<tr><td></td><td></td><td>◀ **Winners**</td><td></td><td></td></tr>
<tr><td>1</td><td>4</td><td>3</td><td>9</td><td>5</td></tr>
<tr><td>10</td><td>7</td><td>8</td><td>2</td><td>6</td></tr>
<tr><td></td><td></td><td>**Losers** ▶</td><td></td><td></td></tr>
<tr><td>4</td><td>3</td><td>2</td><td>5</td><td>6</td></tr>
<tr><td>1</td><td>10</td><td>7</td><td>8</td><td>9</td></tr>
<tr><td>3</td><td>2</td><td>5</td><td>6</td><td>9</td></tr>
<tr><td>1</td><td>4</td><td>10</td><td>7</td><td>8</td></tr>
<tr><td>2</td><td>5</td><td>6</td><td>8</td><td>9</td></tr>
<tr><td>1</td><td>3</td><td>4</td><td>10</td><td>7</td></tr>
<tr><td>3</td><td>4</td><td>8</td><td>7</td><td>9</td></tr>
<tr><td>1</td><td>2</td><td>5</td><td>6</td><td>10</td></tr>
<tr><td>2</td><td>5</td><td>6</td><td>9</td><td>10</td></tr>
<tr><td>1</td><td>3</td><td>4</td><td>8</td><td>7</td></tr>
</table>

Figure 6.5 Level rotation tournament.

do seeds 7, 8, and 9. Players who won move to the left. In the second round the same process occurs again. After several rounds, players are playing those of like ability. There is no ultimate winner or loser, but obviously players would try to move as far to the winners' side as possible.

If there is an insufficient number of playing areas, you could insert a rest area between two playing areas.

Tournament Construction

Whatever means you chose to construct these tournaments, make sure there are sufficient spaces to accommodate the participants. Because you can construct the layouts for these tournaments in a way that makes them reusable, it is usually best to build them for a large number of participants. Here are four ways of constructing layouts for these tournaments.

Bulletin Board

You can place the tournament format on a bulletin board, using cardboard, felt, or other materials to outline the tournament. You can make little cardboard markers identifying the participants and place them appropriately on the board. Due to the amount of player movement that usually occurs during a tournament, it would be wise to use pins that you can easily insert and remove. The disadvantage is that the bulletin board is usually permanently attached to a wall, and its location may not be advantageous in relation to tournament playing areas, or it may be unprotected when not in use—which might result in accidental or intentional alteration.

Portable Board

This board should be large enough to accommodate the number of participants. Usually hooks are placed on the board. Small disks identifying the participants have holes so you can place these disks on the hooks. Another way to make participant identifiers is to use strips of cardboard or tongue depressors. This method of construction is much the same as for the bulletin board, but it has the advantage of portability.

Plastic or Laminated Surface

You can draw the tournament format with permanent markers on a sheet of paper, laminate it, then affix it to a firm material (e.g., wood or cardboard). You can write participants' names using water-soluble markers. This is probably the most flexible method, though it can be messy. A less messy, but more expensive, system is to use erasable marker boards.

Blackboard

You can use blackboards to draw tournaments of short duration. You can make up tournaments quickly and change them as necessary. However, blackboards also are not protected when not in use, which may result in accidental or intentional alteration.

CHAPTER 7

Large Tournaments

■ It is best to think of a large tournament as a series of smaller divisions. Some divisions will occur naturally. For example, you might receive 100 entries for a high school badminton tournament, but they are divided into five categories: men's singles and doubles, women's singles and doubles, and mixed doubles. There may also be a junior and senior division, making 10 different tournaments with an average of 10 entries per category. You would then prepare an appropriate format for each category.

However, you might also encounter a situation in which you have many teams in one category. Perhaps a large two-on-two basketball tournament may have 100 entries. One solution would be to divide these 100 entries into 16 pools resulting in 12 pools of six teams and 4 pools of seven teams. Each entry would play the other entries in their pool. You would place the top two finishers from each pool (a total of 32) on a different single-elimination play-off draw, so these two entries would not meet again unless they made it to the championships. Seed entries so each number one finisher plays a second-place finisher from pool play. Each single-elimination draw would end up with a winner and a second-place finisher. The second-place finishers from the two draws would play for third and fourth overall. The two first-place finishers from the two draws would play in the championship match for first and second overall. The total number of games to complete this whole tournament are as follows:

Pool play

12 pools of 6

$12 ((6 \cdot (6 - 1))/2) = 180$ games

4 pools of 7

$4 ((7 \cdot (7 - 1))/2) = 84$ games

Single-elimination play-offs

$2 (16 - 1) = 30$

Consolation and championships $= 2$ games

Total $= 296$ games

If you had 24 courts it would take

17 rounds to complete pool play,

4 rounds to complete the play-offs,

1 round to complete the consolation and championship game, and

22 rounds to complete the tournament.

If each game took 1/2 hour, the tournament would last 11 hours and the fewest games anyone would play would be five.

There are other options as well. Permit the following personal example. After having tried various pyramid tournaments for squash at our college, we found that not all of the 50 people who signed up were getting involved. We then set up a ladder tournament in which we indicated what entry each person would play that week. We would then move the winners up and losers down accordingly.[1] This did not work when we got to midterms and at the end of the semester when papers were due; one week was too short and contributed to too many defaults. We wanted to give people more time to get their matches in so we went to a series of pools set up in a pyramid fashion. There were five people to a pool, and they were to play each other once each during a four-week period. We would then move the winners to a higher pool and the losers to a lower pool.[2] Students and faculty being what they are, they procrastinated till the last week, then could not get all their games in; one month was too long and contributed to too many defaults. We went to smaller pools of three people per pool, arranging one pool on top of the other. This meant participants needed to get two matches in during two weeks, after which winners would move to the pool above, losers would move to the pool below, and those in the middle stayed.[3] This worked for most people, except those who were on the bottom of a ladder looking at 50 people who were on top of them; those on the bottom began defaulting their games because there seemed little possibility of advancing up the ladder.

We switched to a round robin-pyramid tournament, and this one seems to be working for now. We place participants in pools of three or four people and expect them to get their games in within two weeks. Place these pools in a group of pyramids with the top pool being identified as AAAA, the next group of pyramids as AAA, then AA, and finally A. Rather than placing these groups under each

[1] John Byl, "Formalizing a Ladder Tournament," *NIRSA Journal* 15, no. 1 (fall 1990): 41-43.

[2] John Byl, "A Round Robin Pyramid," *NIRSA Journal* 16, no. 2 (winter 1992): 41-42.

[3] John Byl, "A Round Robin Ladder Tournament," *CAHPER Journal* 60, no. 2 (summer 1994): 25-27.

other, we place them slightly below and to the right of the stronger group. Players at the different levels compete to move up in their respective pyramid, then on to the next one. This approach appears to provide the right incentives for people at all the levels to stay involved. We post a sign-up sheet beside the tournament draw so new people can sign up (they are on the bottom), and those involved can indicate if they wish to withdraw after the current round of play. If someone does not participate for two full rounds of play, I usually withdraw their name from the tournament. If I remove someone from the tournament, entries below the withdrawn entry simply move up one rung. The pool sheets are included on pages 144-147. They are all set up for the AAAA group; to produce the other groups, simply photocopy the master and white out one of the letters to produce sheets for the next group. You may find this round robin-pyramid tournament will work for you. If it does not work, experiment till you find a format that best helps your participants.

Pool   Single-elimination play-offs   Championships

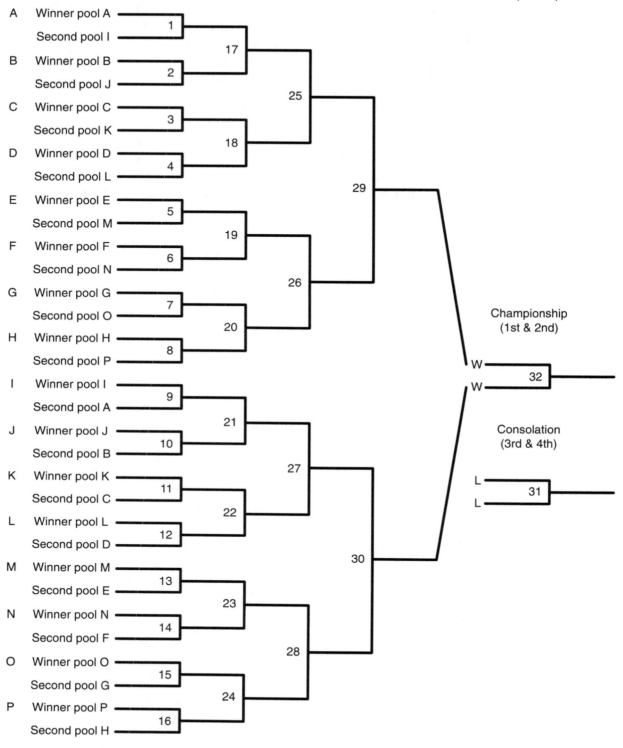

Figure 7.1   Single-elimination schematic.

AAAA

<-- 1st to CCCCC1c
<-- 2nd to CCCCC2c

3rd to BBBB2a-->
<-- 4th to BBBB1a

Names	A	B	C	D	Wins	Place
A _____ _____ _____ _____		a - b a - b a - b a - b a - b	a - c a - c a - c a - c a - c	a - d a - d a - d a - d a - d		
B _____ _____ _____ _____	b - a b - a b - a b - a b - a		b - c b - c b - c b - c b - c	b - d b - d b - d b - d b - d		
C _____ _____ _____ _____	c - a c - a c - a c - a c - a	c - b c - b c - b c - b c - b		c - d c - d c - d c - d c - d		
D _____ _____ _____ _____	d - a d - a d - a d - a d - a	d - b d - b d - b d - b d - b	d - c d - c d - c d - c d - c			

From Organizing Successful Tournaments, 2nd ed. by John Byl, 1999, Champaign, IL: Human Kinetics. Copyright 1999 by John Byl.

BBBB 1

1st to AAAAc ↑

Names	A	B	C	Wins	Place
A _____ _____		a - b a - b a - b a - b a - b	a - c a - c a - c a - c a - c		
B _____ _____	b - a b - a b - a b - a b - a		b - c b - c b - c b - c b - c		
C _____ _____	c - a c - a c - a c - a c - a	c - b c - b c - b c - b c - b			

3rd to CCCC2a-->

CCCC 1

1st to BBBB1c ↑

Names	A	B	C	Wins	Place
A _____ _____		a - b a - b a - b a - b a - b	a - c a - c a - c a - c a - c		
B _____ _____	b - a b - a b - a b - a b - a		b - c b - c b - c b - c b - c		
C _____ _____	c - a c - a c - a c - a c - a	c - b c - b c - b c - b c - b			

3rd to AAAa-->

From Organizing Successful Tournaments, 2nd ed. by John Byl, 1999, Champaign, IL: Human Kinetics. Copyright 1999 by John Byl.

1st to AAAAd ↑

Names	A	B	C	Wins	Place
A _____ _____		a - b a - b a - b a - b a - b	a - c a - c a - c a - c a - c		
B _____ _____	b - a b - a b - a b - a b - a		b - c b - c b - c b - c b - c		
C _____ _____	c - a c - a c - a c - a c - a	c - b c - b c - b c - b c - b			

<-- **3rd to CCCC1a**

1st to BBBB2c ↑

Names	A	B	C	Wins	Place
A _____ _____		a - b a - b a - b a - b a - b	a - c a - c a - c a - c a - c		
B _____ _____	b - a b - a b - a b - a b - a		b - c b - c b - c b - c b - c		
C _____ _____	c - a c - a c - a c - a c - a	c - b c - b c - b c - b c - b			

3rd to AAAb-->

From Organizing Successful Tournaments, 2nd ed. by John Byl, 1999, Champaign, IL: Human Kinetics. Copyright 1999 by John Byl.

CHAPTER 8

Seeding and Byes

■ The concepts of seeding and byes are important to understand in preparing a successful tournament. This manual has prepared seeding charts, which include byes, for each type of tournament, adding ease and accuracy to the tournament director's job. However, if you want to understand how to do seeding, this

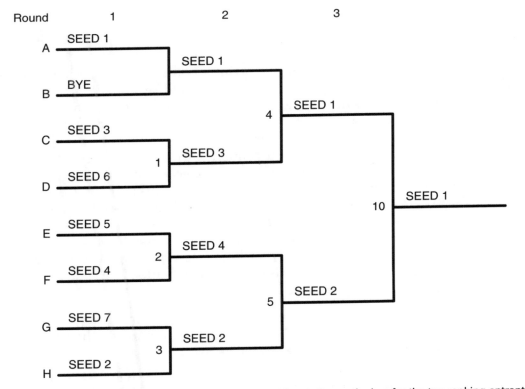

Figure 8.1 Single-elimination tournament with equitable seeding and a bye for the top ranking entrant.

chapter will interest you. Also, for the situation in which it is helpful to seed but the entries have not played each other, this chapter concludes with suggestions for dealing with that.

Byes

The first round of a single-elimination, double-elimination, or multilevel tournament is always calculated to the next-higher perfect power of two. In other words, the initial round allows for up to 2, 4, 6, 16, 32, or 64 entries. You might ask, what happens if I have fewer than that? What happens if I have seven entries? Obviously, the format permitting only four entries would be too small, so a format using eight entries would be necessary. This means that one entry will not have anyone to play in the first round; therefore, that entry receives what is called a *bye*.

Two principles are usually applied in awarding a bye. First, the number one seed or the higher seeds should be overcome by skillful play, not by the exhaustion that can come from a difficult schedule. Second, lower caliber players benefit most from more experience and playing with those of similar ability. Therefore, byes are usually awarded to the higher ranked entries. We illustrate this in figure 8.1, using a single-elimination draw sheet for seven entries. If you are preparing a single-elimination tournament with six entries, then two entries receive byes. These should be the number one and number two seeds.

The process of awarding byes is slightly different in round robin play. In a regular round robin, when there is an odd number of entries, each entry has one bye built into the schedule. In the case of split round robins, if the pools are not all the same size, entries in smaller pools play fewer games; these are not normally referred to as byes, but byes are essentially what those entries are receiving.

Seeding

As stated in chapter 1, in organizing a tournament, especially an elimination tournament, two important principles should be at work in preparing the draw. The first is that the top two entries should meet in the final game; the logical extension of this is that the higher an entry is ranked, the closer it should come to the final game before being eliminated.

A second principle, which is applied differently depending on the seeding philosophy you adopt, is that it should be equally difficult for entries of similar ability to achieve similar ends. Let's illustrate this point with a tournament of 16 entries. Using the equitable seeding approach, the 1st seed competes with the 11th seed, and the 2nd seed competes with the 12th seed—both 10 seeds apart. Using the advantage seeding approach, the 1st seed competes with the 16th, and the 2nd seed competes with the 15th; the higher seed playing the easiest competitor, the second seed playing the second easiest competitor. The benefits of the equitable seeding approach are as follows:

- The weaker teams should have more meaningful games—even though they will still likely be out in the same round as if they were participating in an advantage seeded tournament.
- There should be fewer and less lopsided games than in an advantage seeded tournament.

The benefit of the advantage seeding approach is as follows:

- The stronger teams have earned (usually as the result of previous league or round robin competition) an easier path to their final games, and these earnings are accommodated with this seeding approach.

The easiest way to understand seeding is to apply these two principles from the end of a tournament format to its beginning. Figure 8.1 illustrates this using the equitable seeding approach. Seed 1 should win this tournament and therefore is placed at the end as the winner. To achieve that, seed 1 should have played seed 2 in the final game; seed 1 and seed 2 represent the winners of the two similar brackets, so advance to play each other. The semifinals should include four teams; remaining consistent with our first principle, this should include the top four entries. Who the first and second seeds play is decided by the second principle; seed 1 would play seed 3, and seed 2 would play seed 4. If we did this differently, and seed 1 played seed 4 while seed 2 played seed 3, the top seed would have the advantage of an easier game.

Going to the first round, seed 1 is awarded a bye, and seeds 5, 6, and 7 are added to the draw sheet. If you use the principles consistently, the following would occur: Seed 3 would play seed 6, seed 4 would play seed 7, and seed 2 would play seed 5. Each entry would play someone three seeds away from them, but this would create a considerable disadvantage for seeds 5 and 6. The difference between the fourth and fifth seeds, or for that matter between the fourth and sixth seeds, may not be very much. However, the only way the fifth seed can break into the semifinals, if we seeded as suggested, would be by defeating an entry seeded three levels ahead. Therefore, we altered the seeding for the fifth, sixth, and seventh seeds as indicated in figure 8.1.

Figure 8.2 indicates how improper seeding will lead to an unjust process and unjust results. With respect to the first principle, the top two seeds did make it to the finals, but in the semifinals, round 2, seed 6 made it to the semifinals but seed 3 did not; if the seeding was correct, this would be an undesirable result. With respect to the second principle, a quick look at the playing schedules for the top two seeds indicates a discrepancy. In the case of the second seed, a bye is awarded, a game is played with the sixth seed, then the second seed is into the finals. By contrast, the top seed played the third seed, then the fourth seed, then played the second seed in the finals. Obviously seed 1 had a much more difficult schedule than seed 2 did, and that is likely to be a disadvantage to seed 1.

The process for seeding a multilevel tournament is somewhat different. Once again, you could take a preestablished draw sheet and work your way back. However, if you did not have the advantage of such a draw sheet, you would prepare one as suggested here and illustrated in figure 8.3. If the number of entries is eight, the first objective is to seed in such a way that the top four seeds advance in category A and the bottom four seeds drop to category C. Following this, you want half the entries to stay in the category they are in and half to drop one level. In the case of eight entries, this would bring you to the final game in each category.

Occasionally you may not have the information to know the caliber of each entry, and specific seeding would be difficult. The best solution to this problem is to rank the top quarter of the entries, then divide the remaining entries in half, classifying one group as average, the other weak. For example, suppose there are eight entries and you can clearly identify the top two. You can divide the

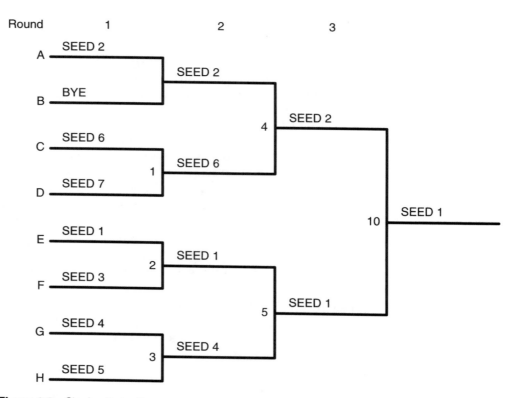

Figure 8.2 Single elimination tournament with improper seeding.

remaining six into two groups: three in the average group and three in the weak group. Place the three in the average group on the draw sheet where the third, fourth, and fifth seed would be; then place the weak group on the draw sheet where the sixth, seventh, and eighth seed would be. It is especially important to seed the top teams correctly and to seed the remaining entries as best as possible.

We must add that, in some sports and leagues, rules specify that the tournament director may seed only a certain number of entries and must simply place the remaining entries onto the draw sheet at random. For example, international badminton regulations do not permit seeding more than 2 entries when there are fewer than 16 players, and no more than 4 entries when the total is less than 32. Eight seeded entries are the maximum allowed.

Using the seeding tables in this manual, or tables you have developed, you may have scheduled two players from the same club or city to play each other. On most

Multilevel seeding			
1 7	2 8	3 5	4 6
1 3	2 4	5 7	6 8
1 2	3 4	5 6	7 8
A	B	C	D

Figure 8.3 Multilevel seeding chart.

occasions this is undesirable, and you may need to slightly modify the seeding order by placing these players in different brackets, pools, or divisions.

Seeding Entries Who Have Not Played Each Other

It is always helpful to seed entries to minimize mismatches and to allow for the top four teams to meet in the semi-finals and the top two teams to meet in the finals. If seeding is based on a season of play, the final league standings provide the basis of seeding. However, it commonly occurs that a tournament convener may be hosting a tournament in which the entries have not played each other. If this is the case, how does one seed the entries?

The most likely place for this situation to occur is in a pre-season exhibition tournament. Another likely situation is for a championship competition in which the entries typically have local competitions advancing a winner to regional or larger tournaments. Examples of the latter include high school provincial or state tournaments or Olympic competitions.

A typical safeguard in each of these situation is to provide a preliminary round of round-robin pool play. For example, if one had 16 entries, one might want to divide the entries into four pools of four. Based on the results of pool play one could then seed a 16-entry single elimination playoff.

But even if one used this safeguard, how could a tournament convener try to insure the best match-ups even in pool play? There would basically be three ways to try and do this:

1. See how these teams did in games they may have played with each other, or with another team.
2. Evaluate historical patterns.
3. Ask around.

If teams have played each other before the tournament then those results can factor into the seeding. Two teams may not have played each other, but they both may have played another team. How the two teams did against the other team can indicate relative strength. If the Lions beat the Bears, and the Bears beat the Cougars, and the Lions and the Cougars are coming to the same tournament, the Lions would be seeded higher than the Cougars.

Historically some teams have very good teams every year and this can be used for ranking purposes. Similarly, teams from certain locations traditionally may be strong or weak in certain sports and this can be used for ranking purposes. Also, if a number of teams coming to the tournament did not play in previous tournaments, their rankings from the previous year can be used. A problem with this is that the caliber of school teams can change quickly when, for example, a lot of players graduate in a particular year.

A tournament convener should also be willing to ask around to see how teams are doing. Coaches could be asked to comment on their team's relative strength from previous years. Coaches may also be able to comment on what they have heard about other teams.

Probably no one approach will solve the problem of accurate seeding for teams that have not played each other for a considerable time. However, all that is asked of tournament conveners is that they do the best they are able. Providing a preliminary round of pool play is probably the safest thing to do. In addition, a more careful look at the entries' history of play will also help make for a good tournament.

A tournament director does seeding with the best information and intentions, but even so there may be upsets. That is part of the fun of the tournament. As tournament director you need not feel bad about that. Rather, you ought to feel good about preparing and hosting a tournament that you have seeded as fairly as possible.

CHAPTER 9

Planning and Conducting Tournaments

■ It is the tournament director's responsibility to ensure that the tournament will run efficiently for all involved—players, officials, and spectators alike. Selecting the appropriate tournament type, and seeding accurately, will help. However, there are many other administrative activities that can make a tournament run smoothly. Many times an association will specify some activities, for example, when participants need to submit entry forms or when you should mail tournament schedules. These associations often specify tiebreaking procedures and other items relevant for a smooth-running tournament. If these items have not been prepared, the following guidelines will prove useful.

For large tournaments, it will be helpful to delegate work to various committees that report back to the tournament director or tournament executive committee. For smaller tournaments, the director may be able to run the tournament with help from select people. For very small tournaments, a director may organize and administer the entire tournament. We have provided a checklist (see figure 9.1) so you can check off items as they are completed. The time line is suitable for a midsize tournament, and you will need to lengthen or shorten it depending on your tournament size.

Avoiding Problems

Adequate planning and getting things done early are crucial to avoiding problems when organizing tournaments. The tournament checklist (figure 9.1) should help you stay on time and plan properly. A few additional words of advice may further minimize potential problems.

You will need to adjust the time line in figure 9.1 according to the nature of your tournament. For large tournaments you should begin organizing much sooner; for less formal tournaments the time constraints are not as applicable. In any large tournament for which you are using committees, you should activate them from the start.

Obtain a written confirmation of facility bookings as early as possible. Without it, no scheduling can really begin, and having it in writing avoids misunderstandings with the facility director.

Based on the number of entries and the objectives of your tournament, you can select a playing schedule from the previous chapters. Then you can develop an appropriate time schedule for tournament day.

Next, you need to book all officials. Do this early, or you risk not acquiring the quality of officials you want; worse yet, you may find none available. Schedule major officials, first aid personnel, and any official security personnel at one time.

Once you've made these arrangements, advise teams of the tournament details: playing schedule, tiebreaking procedures, specific equipment usages (e.g., in badminton the type of shuttlecock to use). It is also helpful to provide maps showing clearly the locations of the playing facility, suitable accommodations, and restaurants. Two maps may be required: a large-scale map showing major routes to the playing site and a small-scale map showing the local area. After you've put in the time to produce this information once, you can copy it for subsequent tournaments.

Participants also need to know what will be provided or available at the tournament, such as game or practice balls, refreshments, towels, first aid equipment or personnel, and snack bar or cafeteria. List costs for any of these items. The more information that is available to participants at this stage, the fewer disappointments there will be on tournament day, and all involved can concentrate their energies on play.

If regulation equipment and awards are not on hand, that would require immediate attention. You cannot always buy an official game ball on short notice, so save yourself the heartache and get it early. Awards also take time to prepare; it is important to acquire them early so if there is an error you have time to make the necessary correction.

Once you've taken care of these details, you can catch your breath before the next major push. A couple weeks before the tournament, arrange minor officials and other personnel. Distribute a schedule to the officials along with a list of their respective duties. If any officials need training, this is the time to do it. Advise janitorial staff of the tournament so that enough supplies are on hand; extra personnel may be needed to help clean the site during and after the tournament.

Make sure you inform the media of your event so they can make plans to cover it. Media may be the local newspaper or simply the school photography club, but you should notify them well in advance.

Sufficient scoring forms need to be on hand. Checking that the score clock functions properly is wise at this time.

1. As soon as possible, and at least a month before the tournament day, the director should
   - ❏ Obtain permission to use, and book, necessary facilities.
   - ❏ Prepare a schedule of play.
   - ❏ Obtain qualified major and minor officials, plus appropriate medical personnel.
   - ❏ Send information about the tournament to all teams involved. This should include a playing schedule, a list of special things to bring to the tournament such as practice balls and, where appropriate, information regarding such things as maps of playing facilities, accommodation information, and food information.
   - ❏ Ensure that regulation equipment is available.
   - ❏ Ensure that awards are ready and that perpetual trophies will be on hand.

2. At least two weeks before the tournament, the director should
   - ❏ Advise media of the event.
   - ❏ Ensure that adequate supervision will be ready for security and crowd control.
   - ❏ Ensure that all scoring forms are ready.
   - ❏ Ensure that all officials know their duties.
   - ❏ Draw up any necessary tournament committees.

3. The last few days before the tournament, the director should
   - ❏ Ensure that appropriate signs are made up identifying such places as change rooms to be used for teams and the location of the cafeteria.

4. On the day of the tournament, the director should
   - ❏ Do a final check to make sure everything is in place.
   - ❏ Hold a coaches' meeting prior to the event to advise coaches of any last-minute concerns and to answer any questions.
   - ❏ Ensure that all personnel are doing their jobs.
   - ❏ Convene a committee to resolve any questions or disputes that might arise from the tournament.

5. Immediately following the tournament, the director should
   - ❏ Prepare and send out an appropriate media release concerning the tournament.

6. Within a week of the tournament, the director should
   - ❏ Prepare and send a report to the participating teams and where necessary to senior conveners and executive directors. This report should contain
     - a. a summary of the tournament results, including matches, games, and so on and final results,
     - b. a report on any meetings held in connection with the tournament,
     - c. an expense report, and
     - d. recommendations for future tournaments.

Figure 9.1 Tournament checklist.

A few days ahead, arrange for signs to be prepared that identify the tournament; tell which teams use which change rooms; and direct participants to the gym, bleachers, cafeteria, first aid room, and change rooms.

The day before the tournament, perform a final check of the facility, the equipment, and the signs to make sure everything is ready to roll.

Come in early on tournament day. In spite of good planning, there are often last-minute items that will need your attention. Make a walk-through of the playing site, checking for anything that might be dangerous to the participants and making sure that nets and lines are officially placed, signs are in place, score sheets and extra pencils are at the score table, the score clock is working, and anything else that needs attention gets it.

Before the first game is to begin you should address three groups of people: the coaches, the athletes, and the spectators. These people are all your guests; remember to treat them that way. Hold a coaches' meeting well before the first game; providing beverages is a thoughtful gesture. Advise coaches of any last-minute concerns and answer any questions they have. If you have not established a protest committee, this is a good opportunity to do so.

Address athletes and spectators early enough to permit sufficient warm-up time for those playing in the first game. Welcome everyone, and summarize key tournament rules, safety considerations, and any other appropriate points. After a brief word of encouragement, the tournament begins.

Wouldn't it be pleasant if on tournament day you could just sit back and enjoy the day? That is a luxury you won't be free to experience. Your advance planning will certainly make a difference in how hectic things are, but at the least it is your job to make sure your guests are well attended to and all things run as smoothly and as timely as possible. This means monitoring the facility, the officials, the support personnel, the spectators, the schedule, and the clock. You probably will not be able to take in much of the playing action. Because a lot of supervision will be needed on tournament day, it is best to remain clear of as much other work as possible, even scoring the results. Trying to wear two caps, such as the tournament director and a coach, is likely to be unsatisfying; you will undoubtedly short-change your team and your tournament guests.

You'll want to decide in advance whether to schedule a closing ceremony; some tournaments lend themselves better than others to having one. Unless it is a key game ending the season or a series, participants usually want to return home as soon as possible. If you do host a closing ceremony, be sure to have all necessary results at your disposal as well as any awards you will be giving. If you want to have a celebrity present the awards, arrange this well in advance. You act as the emcee, making sure that people are properly introduced. Keep the ceremony moving quickly, but do permit sufficient time for award winners to enjoy their moments in the spotlight.

As the tournament comes to a close, make sure that teams are safely on their way home, officials have been paid, equipment has been returned to its appropriate places, and the playing site has been left in its original condition. Informally thank participants and officials as they leave. Depending on the association or media you are dealing with, a tournament summary may need to go out that day. Finally, after a busy and satisfying day, it is time to go home.

Participants and associations like nothing better than getting a tournament summary as soon as possible. If you have the use of a personal computer, you can create much of the report and the cover letter before the tournament begins. Then, when the tournament is over, all that is required is to enter some information and do minor editing, and you are ready to distribute the report.

Remember to send an official note of appreciation to the officials and others who helped organize and implement the tournament. The gesture is an appropriate courtesy, and it may help you when you need some of these people for your next tournament.

All the schedules in this book assume that you are using only one draw. However, in some sports, such as badminton and tennis, there will be different divisions—for example, men's singles, women's singles, men's doubles, women's doubles, and mixed doubles. At times there may be additional categories for junior and senior players. Usually these events are held at separate times and often on separate days. For example, singles will be held on the first day, and doubles will be held on the early part of the second day, followed by mixed doubles. This method is usually preferred when players can enter two or more categories. If entries are limited to one event, then the preferred method is to alternate the categories in a balanced way. Alternating the categories, with, for instance, men's singles playing one round, followed by a round of women's singles, and so on, gives greater opportunity for participants to receive adequate rest between matches.

When preparing a schedule, the tournament director should also keep in mind the best arrival time for the different entries. If two entries are of nearly equal caliber, but one has a greater distance to travel, then the one closer to the playing site should play the earlier game.

Committee Responsibilities

For large tournaments, delegating work to committees will be helpful. The following committees should be sufficient to ensure that work is evenly divided and that all tasks of organizing a successful tournament will be properly completed:

Tournament director(s)

Participant publicity and services

Officials and playing equipment

Spectator publicity, services, and control

Awards

Finance

The tournament director is responsible for running the entire tournament. This person or committee bids for the tournament, prepares the draw, and constantly supervises all aspects of the tournament to ensure that it is successfully organized and implemented.

The other committees must complete their work and report to the tournament director any decisions they have made as well as progress they are making on fulfilling their responsibilities. In the early stages, each committee ought to prepare a budget and submit it to the finance committee. When the tournament is completed, each committee needs to submit a final report to the tournament director. This report should include a summary of the committee's work and recommendations for future tournaments.

The participant publicity and services committee is responsible for publicizing the tournament, inviting entries to register, registering the entries, and providing entries with the necessary pretournament and tournament-day services. Pretournament services include directions to the playing site and information regarding accommodations and food. Some large tournaments may involve the additional work of providing accommodations. Tournament-day services include such things as on-site refreshments, medical services, game-time amenities, and informational signs. If a tournament banquet is being provided, this committee should also prepare and host it.

The officials and playing equipment committee's first task is to acquire the services of appropriately certified officials; in the case of minor officials this committee may need to hold several training sessions so these officials will do their jobs correctly. This committee's second task is to ensure that regulation equipment is on hand and that the playing area is properly in place, with fields lined, benches in place, and so on. This committee should also acquire and place score sheets, clocks, and other necessary officiating equipment.

The spectator publicity, services, and control committee is primarily concerned with the spectators. Spectators are those who come to watch the game as well as anyone who is interested in hearing about it later. This committee should arrange for adequate seating and refreshment concessions for those who watch. This committee should also administer security to ensure the safety and enjoyment of the spectators and athletes as well as the protection of the playing facility.

The awards committee is responsible for acquiring appropriate awards. They should also organize the presentation of these awards; this involves deciding who will determine the award winners, who will present the awards, and when they should present the awards.

The finance committee will prepare an overall budget for the tournament and control the funds throughout the tournament. They will be responsible for paying all the bills. They will also be responsible for collecting gate receipts.

The Tournament Director and the Law*

The safety of participants is vital to staging successful tournaments. The law asks you to plan and implement your tournament as well as any reasonable and prudent tournament director would. Proper planning, adequate and competent supervision, a safe playing site, and written records are instrumental to ensuring a safe tournament for all and protecting yourself from litigation.

Obviously the playing site needs to be safe for all concerned. If a field will be played on, carefully walk the field, looking for any potholes, protruding objects, or rocks that need to be dealt with before play begins. Do this walk several days in advance and on the tournament day. A written record of both walks should include when you completed the walk, how you did it, and any findings and actions taken. If fields are to be lined, use field marking chalk or talc powder; avoid lime because it can burn if it contacts the eyes or an open wound.

Follow the same procedures at an indoor site. It would also be wise to prepare a thorough checklist to file with any recommendations for action and a record of follow-up. Just before the tournament, use the list again, with special attention to the areas required for the tournament. Figure 9.2 provides an example of such a form for volleyball.

To further decrease the likelihood of injury, use equipment that is up to standard. Adhere to official rules in preparing the playing site. Standard equipment (such as padding for volleyball posts) is imperative. Rule books for most sports state how far the team bench needs to be from the sideline or how much room is needed from the edge of the court to the wall. If the wall is too close, install proper padding to the floor—players must not be able to strike the wall when running or sliding into it. Any objects protruding from the wall that may endanger athletes must be padded. At the beginning of the tournament, advise

---

*For a more detailed understanding of sport law, read *Coaches Guide of Sport Law* by Gary Nygaard and Thomas Boone (Champaign, IL: Human Kinetics, 1985).

Date of check _____

Time of check _____

Name of checker _____

	Okay	Needs attention	Remarks
Playing site			
All lights are working.	_____	_____	_____
All lights are covered with protective screens.	_____	_____	_____
Portable equipment is at least 20 feet from the court.	_____	_____	_____
Protruding hazards are adequately padded.	_____	_____	_____
Spectator and off-court player movement will not interfere with play.	_____	_____	_____
Volleyball concerns			
Net is in good repair.	_____	_____	_____
Net is at regulation height.	_____	_____	_____
Ball is inflated to regulation pressure.	_____	_____	_____
Support posts are adequately padded.	_____	_____	_____
Score table is a safe distance from the court.	_____	_____	_____
Team benches are a safe distance from the court.	_____	_____	_____
Towels are available to wipe spills from refreshment containers.	_____	_____	_____

Figure 9.2 Safe-site checklist for volleyball.

participants of potential dangers and the precautions you have taken to minimize injuries.

Spectator safety is important as well. Seating should be structurally safe and provide adequate protection from balls, especially if a sport is new to the community.

You may want to cordon off particular areas (for example, to avoid spectator and athlete contact), and advise people to remain in their designated spaces. Depending on the likely emotional intensity of the contest, you may need to arrange for appropriate security. You may feel you should rope off some exits for crowd control. However, in case of fire this can be deadly because people cannot exit quickly; therefore, you need to exercise considerable caution if you do so.

Verify that the institution sponsoring the tournament is adequately insured. Insurance should cover you as director and all participants (including officials, players, spectators, and support personnel) at any location you are using for the tournament. It may be wise to distribute accountability for the safety of all participants by having participants, or a legal representative of a participating team, sign a waiver form along with the entry. Figures 9.3 and 9.4 are samples of such forms. This form does not, however, protect you against negligent behavior. You should be aware that a parent or guardian cannot sign away the rights of a child; a child could be represented by a lawyer who would file suit in the child's name.

First aid procedures, supplies, and personnel need to be in place and accessible on tournament day. It has been suggested that anyone who coaches should be able to administer first aid, including cardiopulmonary resuscitation, and maintain current certification. The same could be said for you as tournament director. Procedures for dealing with injuries must be clearly defined in writing and understood by all concerned. These procedures should include such details as responsibilities of personnel, the location of the nearest telephone, emergency numbers, the extent and nature of treatment permitted, and the necessity for filing a follow-up report. Once again documentation is important. You can use the National Safety Council's "Standard Student Activity Form" when recording this information.

Screening entries is a factor in tournament safety; highly unbalanced players or teams are undesirable. I have observed a novice badminton player lose the eyesight in one eye after playing a tournament game against an experienced opponent. Had this mismatch not occurred, the injury would have been less likely. Either limit your entrants to those of similar caliber or choose a tournament type that will quickly separate novices from experienced players. This will not only be safer for participants, but also will likely provide more meaningful play.

Name _____

Address _____

City _____ State _____ Zip _____

Telephone: Home _____ Business _____

Male _____ Female _____ Birth date _____

T-shirt size: Adult or child

    Sm _____ Med _____ Lg _____

Release form

In consideration of your accepting this entry, I hereby waive all claims against the [sponsor], associated sponsors, and any of their personnel for any injury I might suffer in this event. I hereby attest that I am physically fit and sufficiently prepared for completing the event. Further, I hereby grant full permission for sponsors and organizers to include pictures of me and quotations from me in any legitimate accounts of the [event] and in promotion thereof. If [event] is canceled, my registration fee will be refunded.

Signature _____

Date _____

Figure 9.3 Individual entry form.

We are honored to host the [tournament name], to be held [date] at [site location]. We would like to see your team participate. The fee for the tournament is [$], payable to [name of institution]. If you are interested, please indicate your intent below and return this form and your payment by [date] to

[Registrar or tournament director's name]

[Complete address]

We will be using certified officials and will ensure that the facility is safe to play in. [An/No] athletic trainer will be on hand. As a legal representative of your team, you realize the inherent dangers in this sport and accept responsibility for the conduct of your team. Should one of your players receive an injury, your institution's insurance policy should adequately cover costs incurred.

Team name _____

Coach's name _____

Coach's phone number _____

Team representative _____

Team representative's signature _____

Team representative's position _____

Team representative's year of birth _____

Date signed _____

Figure 9.4 Invitational tournament entry form.

Finally, when tournament day arrives, highlight for participants the important components of your safety plan, noting fire exits, any potential hazards on the playing site, and what to do in case of an injury. If an athletic therapist is available, advise injured participants not to move until he or she arrives.

Concerns over litigation are real and justified, but they should not scare you from taking on the responsibilities of organizing a tournament. If you act reasonably and with prudence, you are not likely to need to defend yourself against a charge of negligence. More importantly, the participants in your tournament will have enjoyed safe play.

A P P E N D I X

Tiebreaking Procedures

From time to time a game needs to have a winner and cannot be left as a tie. The first part of this appendix gives examples of how that can be done. In the case of round robin tournaments or league play it may also be necessary to break a tie for purposes of final standings. The second part of this appendix explains how that can be done.

Tiebreaking Procedures for Games

You should use tiebreaking procedures only when the outcome of a game determines which entry advances or when knowing the final standings is necessary. We have also listed alternative procedures. A common alternative that works for most sports is to advance the entry that scored the first point.

Badminton

Women's singles games go to 11; all other games go to 15. If the score is tied just before the final point, the person who achieved the leading point first chooses whether the game is not set (the game goes on to 11 or 15) or the game is set, which would be as follows:

	Score	Set to
Women	9-9	3
	10-10	2
Men	13-13	5
	14-14	3

Baseball

Play continues until

- the visiting team has scored more total runs than the home team at the end of a completed inning, or
- the home team scores the winning run in an uncompleted inning.

Basketball

- Following a one-minute intermission an extra period is played.
- If the score is still tied, repeat this procedure until the tie is broken.

Alternative.   Using free throw shooting, both teams select five players at the conclusion of the game and alternate free throws. If, before both teams have taken five free throws, one team has scored more than the other, shooting shall cease. If the score is still tied after all 10 players have taken their free throws, this shooting shall continue one player at a time until, after an equal number of shots, one team has scored one more basket than the other.

Football

- Use a 10-minute intermission followed by a 20-minute overtime period of two 10-minute halves.
- If the score is still tied, then use the same procedure but with a 5-minute intermission.

Alternative.   Teams alternate kicking field goals beginning from the 20-yard line. Each time both teams complete their kicks, the ball is taken back an additional 10 yards. If both teams miss, another kick is taken from the same spot. If one team completes the kick and the other fails, the former team wins.

Ice Hockey

- Use a 10-minute intermission followed by a 20-minute sudden-death overtime period.
- If the score is still tied, then use the same procedure until one team scores a goal.

Alternative.   Five players from each team alternate taking penalty shots. Teams can shoot at the same time if both nets are used. The puck is taken from center ice, and the player may stickhandle in and take one shot. If, before both teams have taken five shots, one team has scored more goals than the other could, even if it were to complete its five shots, then shots shall cease. If the score is still tied after all 10 players have shot, shots shall continue one player at a time until, after an equal number of shots, one team has scored one more goal than the other.

Lacrosse, Box

- Use a 10-minute intermission followed by a 10-minute stop-time overtime period.
- Use a 10-minute intermission followed by a 20-minute sudden-death overtime period.
- The last process continues until a goal is scored.

Lacrosse, Field

- Use a 5-minute intermission followed by two 4-minute periods.
- Use a 1-minute intermission followed by 4-minute periods of sudden-death competition.